I0013168

Computer Vision Simplified

Practical Approaches to AI Image Recognition

THOMPSON CARTER

Table of Content

TABLE OF CONTENTS

INTRODUCTION

Unveiling the World of Computer Vision

In an age where artificial intelligence (AI) and machine learning (ML) are shaping the future of technology, **computer vision** stands out as one of the most exciting and transformative fields. From self-driving cars to facial recognition in smartphones, computer vision is behind the systems that allow machines to interpret and understand visual data, just as humans do. This book, **"Computer Vision Simplified: Practical Approaches to AI Image Recognition,"** is designed to take you on a journey through this fascinating field, breaking down complex concepts and making them accessible for both beginners and experienced practitioners alike.

What is Computer Vision?

Computer vision is a subset of AI that empowers machines to see, recognize, and understand the world by processing images, videos, and visual data. Just as the human brain interprets visual information to make decisions and interact with the environment, computer vision enables computers to do the same. From identifying objects in images to understanding complex scenes in video footage, computer vision technologies are now embedded in countless real-world applications, including security, healthcare, automotive systems, and entertainment.

At its core, computer vision involves teaching machines how to extract meaningful information from visual inputs. But beyond just recognizing objects, modern computer vision techniques enable tasks like **image segmentation**, **activity recognition**, and even **generating new images** through models like Generative Adversarial Networks (GANs). As computer vision continues to evolve, the possibilities for its applications are virtually limitless.

Why This Book?

While the theory behind computer vision can often seem daunting, this book aims to break it down into simple, understandable steps that you can apply in real-world projects. Whether you're a beginner looking to understand the fundamentals or an experienced practitioner eager to explore advanced topics, this book will equip you with the knowledge and tools needed to build and deploy powerful computer vision systems.

In these chapters, we'll start with the basics, covering how computer vision works and the core techniques used to recognize and understand images. As we progress, we'll delve into more complex topics like deep learning, neural networks, and advanced architectures that power the most sophisticated computer vision systems today.

What Will You Learn?

Throughout this book, you'll gain hands-on experience and practical insights into the following key areas:

1. **Fundamentals of Computer Vision**: Learn how machines process images, detect objects, and understand scenes. You'll discover the basic algorithms and techniques used in image recognition, classification, and segmentation.

2. **Deep Learning for Image Recognition**: Understand how deep learning has revolutionized the field of computer vision, particularly through Convolutional Neural Networks (CNNs), which have become the gold standard for many image-related tasks.

3. **Real-World Applications**: Explore how computer vision is applied in the real world—from autonomous vehicles and medical imaging to security systems and augmented reality. Through case studies, you'll see how these technologies are transforming industries.

4. **Advanced Topics**: Dive deeper into cutting-edge techniques like transfer learning, object detection with YOLO, image segmentation with Mask R-CNN, and generative models like GANs. These topics will help you stay on the cutting edge of computer vision research.

5. **Building a Computer Vision System from Scratch**: Gain practical experience by building a complete image recognition system. We'll guide you through the process, from collecting and preprocessing data to training models, evaluating performance, and deploying the system.

6. **Emerging Trends and Future Directions**: Stay ahead of the curve by exploring the future of computer vision, including new developments in neural architecture search, self-supervised learning, and quantum computing. We'll discuss the latest research and what lies ahead for this rapidly evolving field.

Who Is This Book For?

This book is designed for anyone interested in learning about computer vision. Whether you're:

- A **beginner** who is just starting to explore machine learning and computer vision.
- An **intermediate practitioner** looking to deepen your knowledge and skills with more advanced topics.
- An **industry professional** seeking practical insights to apply computer vision in real-world projects.

The approach taken in this book is **hands-on** and **practical**. We emphasize building real systems that can be applied to solve real problems. Each chapter contains step-by-step tutorials, real-world examples, and explanations of both the theory and practice behind the techniques discussed.

Why Now? The Growing Impact of Computer Vision

The field of computer vision has experienced explosive growth over the last decade, largely driven by advances in deep learning, the availability of large datasets, and increased computational power. The integration of computer vision into everyday technology has transformed how we interact with the world. Some notable examples include:

- **Autonomous Vehicles**: Cars that can perceive and understand the environment around them, enabling them to navigate and make decisions without human intervention.
- **Medical Imaging**: AI-driven systems that help doctors detect and diagnose diseases from X-rays, MRIs, and other scans with unprecedented accuracy.
- **Retail and E-Commerce**: Product recognition systems that enhance the customer shopping experience by recommending similar products based on visual data.
- **Surveillance Systems**: Real-time monitoring systems that detect anomalies and provide security solutions using facial recognition and activity tracking.

As these technologies continue to evolve, the demand for skilled professionals in computer vision is growing rapidly. Understanding and implementing these technologies not only opens up exciting career opportunities but also allows you to contribute to shaping the future of AI.

Your Path Forward

By the end of this book, you will have the knowledge and tools to develop computer vision systems and apply them to real-world problems. But this is just the beginning of your journey. The field of computer vision is incredibly dynamic, and staying updated with the latest trends and research is key to continuing your development. Whether you decide to specialize in healthcare, autonomous vehicles, or another domain, the foundations covered here will serve as a springboard for your future endeavors in AI and computer vision.

As you progress through this book, you'll learn not only the theory and algorithms behind computer vision but also how to implement them using popular frameworks like **TensorFlow**, **Keras**, **PyTorch**, and **OpenCV**. You'll build real-world systems and gain hands-on experience in applying these technologies to solve problems in industries like healthcare, security, retail, and beyond.

Welcome to the world of computer vision! We're excited to guide you through this journey of learning, building, and innovating. Let's get started on this path toward mastering the art of image recognition and AI-powered vision systems.

CHAPTER 1

Introduction to Computer Vision

What is Computer Vision?

Computer Vision is a multidisciplinary field in artificial intelligence (AI) that focuses on enabling computers and systems to interpret and understand visual information from the world, much like humans do. Essentially, it's the process of teaching machines to see, analyze, and make decisions based on images or video data.

At its core, computer vision involves:

- **Image Acquisition**: Capturing images or videos using cameras or other visual sensors.
- **Image Processing**: Enhancing or transforming raw visual data into a usable format.
- **Feature Extraction**: Identifying key features within an image (edges, shapes, colors, etc.) that help the machine understand the content.
- **Interpretation**: Analyzing the features to recognize patterns, objects, or behaviors.
- **Decision Making**: Using the insights gained from images to make decisions or take actions (e.g., object detection, facial recognition, etc.).

Key Applications in the Real World

1. **Self-Driving Cars**

- One of the most famous and transformative applications of computer vision is in autonomous vehicles. Self-driving cars rely heavily on computer vision for tasks such as:
  - **Object detection**: Identifying pedestrians, other vehicles, and obstacles.
  - **Lane detection**: Recognizing road markings and ensuring the vehicle stays within its lane.
  - **Traffic sign recognition**: Interpreting road signs for speed limits, stop signs, etc.
  - **Traffic light detection**: Understanding the status of traffic signals to ensure safe navigation.
- Example: Tesla's Autopilot system uses computer vision to interpret the surrounding environment, enabling semi-autonomous driving.

2. **Medical Image Analysis**
   - In healthcare, computer vision plays a critical role in diagnosing diseases by analyzing medical images such as X-rays, MRIs, CT scans, and ultrasound images. Some common tasks include:
     - **Tumor detection**: Identifying signs of cancer or abnormal growths in radiological images.
     - **Organ segmentation**: Isolating different organs in medical scans for better diagnosis.

- **Disease classification**: Classifying skin conditions from images to detect diseases like melanoma.
  - Example: AI-powered tools like Google Health's breast cancer detection system have been shown to outperform human doctors in detecting early-stage breast cancer from mammograms.

3. **Facial Recognition**
   - Computer vision is widely used for facial recognition applications, such as unlocking smartphones, verifying identities for security systems, and even in law enforcement to track individuals of interest.
   - Example: Apple's Face ID uses computer vision to recognize and authenticate users by mapping their facial features.

4. **Retail and E-commerce**
   - Computer vision is revolutionizing the retail industry through tools like automated checkouts, visual search engines, and inventory management.
     - **Visual search**: Allowing consumers to search for products by uploading images rather than typing keywords.
     - **Inventory management**: Automated systems that monitor shelf stock and product placement in stores.

- o Example: Amazon Go stores use computer vision, sensors, and deep learning to provide a checkout-free shopping experience.

5. **Agriculture**
   - o Computer vision also plays a vital role in modern agriculture, where it's used for tasks like crop monitoring, pest detection, and yield prediction.
     - **Plant health monitoring**: Using drones equipped with cameras to capture images and detect plant diseases or nutrient deficiencies.
     - **Harvesting robots**: Identifying ripe fruits or vegetables and automating the harvesting process.
   - o Example: John Deere's autonomous tractors use computer vision to plant crops more efficiently and identify potential issues in fields.

Evolution of Computer Vision and AI

Computer vision, as a field, has evolved significantly over the years. Initially, computer vision systems relied on simple techniques, like edge detection and geometric analysis, but advancements in machine learning, particularly deep learning, have propelled the field into new heights.

- **Early Days (1950s–1980s)**: Early computer vision research focused on basic image processing techniques, like object recognition and geometric transformations. Early systems were rule-based and couldn't handle the complexity of real-world visual data.

- **Machine Learning Revolution (1990s–2000s)**: In the 1990s, machine learning algorithms started to be applied to computer vision, allowing systems to learn from data rather than relying solely on hand-crafted rules. However, these systems were still limited by the computational resources available at the time.
- **Deep Learning Era (2010s–Present)**: The major breakthrough in computer vision came with the advent of deep learning, particularly Convolutional Neural Networks (CNNs). These networks can automatically learn hierarchical features from raw image data, improving accuracy and enabling more sophisticated tasks like real-time object detection, facial recognition, and image generation.
  - In 2012, a CNN called **AlexNet** won the ImageNet competition, a key moment in the rise of deep learning. This event marked the beginning of the AI revolution in computer vision.
  - The introduction of **Generative Adversarial Networks (GANs)** further expanded the possibilities of computer vision, enabling the generation of high-quality images from scratch.

A Brief Look at the History and Major Breakthroughs

- **1960s–1970s**: Early computer vision researchers, like Larry Roberts and David Marr, focused on how to process visual data using mathematical models. However, the computational limitations of the time meant that their ideas were mostly theoretical.
- **1980s**: Interest in machine learning grew, and researchers started developing algorithms that could learn from data. Techniques like **template matching** and **feature extraction** were introduced.
- **1990s**: Algorithms like **Support Vector Machines (SVM)** and **k-Nearest Neighbors (k-NN)** began being applied to image recognition. The first face detection algorithms were developed in the 1990s, laying the groundwork for modern facial recognition systems.
- **2000s**: The invention of the **Hough Transform** for detecting objects in images was a major milestone. It allowed systems to detect specific shapes, such as circles and lines, in noisy images.
- **2010s**: The deep learning revolution took off, led by innovations in CNNs and architectures like **ResNet**, **VGG**, and **YOLO**. These models were able to process images with high accuracy and speed, powering modern applications such as self-driving cars and medical diagnosis.
- **2018–Present**: New advancements, like **transformer-based architectures** for vision (e.g., Vision Transformers or ViTs), are leading the next wave of breakthroughs. This approach

has shown promise in achieving even better performance than traditional CNNs on large datasets.

This chapter provides a foundational understanding of computer vision, covering both its conceptual frameworks and practical applications. As you move forward, the following chapters will dive deeper into the techniques and technologies that power these innovations.

CHAPTER 2

Understanding Image Data

In this chapter, we'll dive into the different types of image data, how images are represented at the pixel level, and why preprocessing plays such a crucial role in preparing data for machine learning tasks. Understanding these concepts will set a solid foundation for later chapters where we'll work with real-world image recognition systems.

Types of Images

1. **Grayscale Images**
   - Grayscale images contain only shades of gray, with no color information. Each pixel value represents the intensity of light, with 0 being black and 255 being white (on a scale of 0–255). Grayscale images are often used in scenarios where color isn't important, such as in medical imaging (X-rays, MRIs) or edge detection tasks.
   - **Real-World Example**: A medical scan, such as a CT scan, may be represented as a grayscale image, with different intensities corresponding to various tissue densities.
2. **RGB Images**
   - RGB (Red, Green, Blue) images are the most common type of images in computer vision, especially for tasks involving

color recognition and classification. Each pixel in an RGB image is made up of three values: one for red, one for green, and one for blue. These values determine the color of the pixel.

- o **Real-World Example**: Photographs, social media images, and e-commerce product photos are typically RGB images. Color plays an important role in identifying objects, such as distinguishing between red apples and green apples.

3. **Depth Maps**
   - o Depth maps provide information about the distance between the camera and the objects in the scene. Each pixel in a depth map represents how far away that point in the image is from the camera. Depth information is crucial in applications like 3D scene reconstruction and robotic navigation.
   - o **Real-World Example**: In autonomous vehicles, depth maps created from stereo cameras or LiDAR sensors help the car's system understand how far other vehicles, pedestrians, and obstacles are.

4. **Infrared (IR) Images**
   - o Infrared images capture heat rather than visible light. They are used in low-light or night vision applications where traditional cameras wouldn't work. The pixel values represent the temperature of the objects in the scene.

- o **Real-World Example**: Night vision cameras in surveillance systems or thermal imaging for detecting heat leaks in buildings often use infrared images.

Pixels and Image Resolution

1. **Pixels**
   - o The smallest unit of an image is a **pixel** (short for "picture element"). Each pixel in an image holds color or intensity information (depending on the type of image), and it is the building block of the whole image.
   - o In an RGB image, each pixel has 3 values (Red, Green, Blue), while in a grayscale image, each pixel holds a single value.
2. **Image Resolution**
   - o **Resolution** refers to the amount of detail an image holds, determined by the number of pixels in an image. It's usually represented as width x height (e.g., 1920x1080 pixels). Higher resolution images have more pixels, which can lead to more detailed representations but also require more computational resources to process.
   - o **Real-World Example**: A high-definition (HD) image may have a resolution of 1920x1080, while a low-resolution image could have 640x480 pixels. Higher resolution is important for applications

that require fine details, such as facial recognition or satellite image analysis.

Image Preprocessing: Normalization, Resizing, and Augmentation

Before training any machine learning model on image data, preprocessing is crucial to improve the model's accuracy and reduce computational costs. Below are the primary preprocessing techniques.

1. **Normalization**
   o **Normalization** is the process of scaling the pixel values to a specific range, often 0 to 1 or -1 to 1. This is done by dividing each pixel value by the maximum possible pixel value (e.g., 255 for 8-bit images).
   o Why it's important: Neural networks and machine learning models tend to perform better when the input data is normalized because it makes the training process faster and more stable.
   o **Real-World Example**: In image classification tasks, the pixel values of RGB images are typically normalized so that each pixel's value is between 0 and 1, which helps the model learn more effectively.
2. **Resizing**
   o **Resizing** is the process of changing the dimensions (height and width) of an image, often to match the input

requirements of a model. Many machine learning models, especially convolutional neural networks (CNNs), require that all input images have the same size.

- o Why it's important: Resizing images ensures consistency in input dimensions. It also reduces the computational load by scaling down large images for faster processing.
- o **Real-World Example**: For a CNN trained to classify images of cats and dogs, all images might be resized to 224x224 pixels (a common input size for models like VGG16 or ResNet).

3. **Data Augmentation**
   - o **Data augmentation** is a technique to artificially increase the size of the training dataset by applying random transformations to the images. These transformations include:
     - ▪ **Rotation**: Rotating the image at random angles.
     - ▪ **Flipping**: Horizontally or vertically flipping the image.
     - ▪ **Zooming**: Randomly zooming into the image to simulate varying distances.
     - ▪ **Shifting**: Shifting the image along the x or y axis.
     - ▪ **Shearing**: Applying an affine transformation to skew the image.
   - o Why it's important: Augmentation helps the model generalize better by

introducing more diversity into the training data, which can prevent overfitting.

- o **Real-World Example**: In a dataset of images of vehicles, augmentation can simulate different viewing angles, weather conditions, or lighting variations, which allows the model to recognize vehicles under diverse real-world circumstances.

Real-World Examples of Data Preparation

1. **Preparing Data for Self-Driving Cars**
   - o In the case of self-driving cars, the data preparation process is highly complex. Images from cameras mounted on the car are collected in various lighting and weather conditions. These images are then normalized, resized, and augmented (e.g., adding simulated fog or rain) to prepare the model to recognize pedestrians, other vehicles, road signs, and traffic lights.
2. **Medical Image Analysis**
   - o For medical imaging tasks like tumor detection, preprocessing involves cleaning and normalizing images to account for variations in contrast and brightness. Images may also be augmented by rotating or cropping to simulate different orientations of organs or abnormalities. Additionally,

techniques like image denoising may be applied to improve the quality of noisy medical scans.

3. **Retail and Product Recognition**
   o For e-commerce applications, a product recognition system may involve preprocessing product images to make them uniform in size and orientation. Augmentation can simulate different product placements or lighting conditions, helping the system perform well even if a product appears in different environments during actual use.

This chapter provided a foundational understanding of image data and preprocessing techniques. With this knowledge, you'll be able to properly prepare your image datasets for machine learning tasks. In the upcoming chapters, we'll dive deeper into how to leverage these techniques for various computer vision applications.

## CHAPTER 3

Core Concepts in AI and Machine Learning

In this chapter, we'll cover some fundamental concepts that will form the backbone of the techniques we'll explore in later chapters. We'll start with the key differences between Artificial Intelligence (AI), Machine Learning (ML), and Deep Learning (DL). Then, we'll discuss how machine learning fits into computer vision, the difference between supervised and unsupervised learning, and finally, we'll walk through a hands-on example using a decision tree for image classification.

Difference Between AI, ML, and Deep Learning

1. **Artificial Intelligence (AI)**
   - **Definition**: AI refers to the broad field of creating intelligent agents or systems that can perform tasks that typically require human intelligence. These tasks include problem-solving, decision-making, understanding natural language, and recognizing patterns.
   - **Key Characteristics**:
     - Simulating human-like cognitive functions (learning, reasoning, problem-solving).
     - Can be rule-based or data-driven.

- o **Real-World Example**: Chatbots, autonomous vehicles, and digital assistants (like Siri or Alexa) are examples of AI applications.

2. **Machine Learning (ML)**
   - o **Definition**: Machine Learning is a subset of AI that focuses on building systems that can learn from and make predictions or decisions based on data, without being explicitly programmed.
   - o **Key Characteristics**:
     - ML systems learn from data by recognizing patterns and improving their predictions over time.
     - Involves algorithms like regression, classification, and clustering.
   - o **Real-World Example**: Email spam filters, recommendation systems (like those used by Netflix or Amazon), and fraud detection systems are all powered by ML algorithms.

3. **Deep Learning (DL)**
   - o **Definition**: Deep Learning is a subfield of Machine Learning that uses multi-layered neural networks (also called **deep neural networks**) to model complex patterns in large datasets. It is especially effective in tasks such as image recognition, natural language processing, and speech recognition.
   - o **Key Characteristics**:

- Deep neural networks consist of many layers of neurons that can automatically extract high-level features from raw data, eliminating the need for manual feature engineering.
- It requires large datasets and significant computational power.
  - **Real-World Example**: Image recognition systems like Google Vision and facial recognition technologies like Face ID in Apple products are powered by deep learning.

How Machine Learning Fits into Computer Vision

Computer vision is a branch of AI that focuses on enabling machines to interpret and understand visual data from the world. Machine Learning plays a crucial role in computer vision by helping machines learn how to recognize objects, classify images, and understand visual patterns without human intervention.

- **Image Classification**: ML algorithms, particularly supervised learning models, are trained on labeled image datasets to classify images into different categories (e.g., identifying cats vs. dogs).
- **Object Detection**: ML models like decision trees, random forests, and deep neural networks help identify and locate objects within images.
- **Image Segmentation**: Machine learning algorithms can be used to segment an image into

different regions based on their content (e.g., separating foreground from background).

By using ML algorithms, computer vision systems can automatically improve their accuracy as they are exposed to more data, making them highly effective in real-world applications.

Supervised vs Unsupervised Learning in Image Recognition

1. **Supervised Learning**
   o **Definition**: In supervised learning, the algorithm is trained on a labeled dataset, where each training example is paired with a correct output (label). The algorithm learns to map inputs to the correct output by finding patterns in the labeled data.
   o **For Image Recognition**: Supervised learning is commonly used for tasks such as image classification, where the system learns to recognize specific categories (e.g., dogs, cars, etc.) based on labeled images.
   o **Key Steps**:
     ▪ Train the model on labeled data (input images with known labels).
     ▪ The model makes predictions on new, unseen data.
     ▪ The predictions are compared to the true labels, and the model is adjusted accordingly.

- o **Real-World Example**: A facial recognition system trained on a dataset of labeled images of different people. It learns to recognize faces by analyzing the features (eyes, nose, mouth) and their relationships in labeled images.

2. **Unsupervised Learning**
   - o **Definition**: Unsupervised learning involves training a model on data that does not have labels. The algorithm attempts to find hidden patterns or structures in the data, such as grouping similar images together (clustering).
   - o **For Image Recognition**: Unsupervised learning is used in applications like image clustering, where the goal is to group similar images without pre-defined categories or labels.
   - o **Key Steps**:
     - Provide the algorithm with unlabeled data.
     - The model identifies patterns and structures in the data, such as clusters of similar images.
   - o **Real-World Example**: A system that groups product images based on visual similarity, without knowing beforehand which products belong together (e.g., grouping shoes, clothes, and accessories based on visual features).

3. **Semi-supervised Learning**
   - o **Definition**: A combination of supervised and unsupervised learning, semi-

supervised learning uses a small amount of labeled data along with a large amount of unlabeled data. It is particularly useful when labeling large datasets is expensive or time-consuming.

- o **Real-World Example**: A machine learning model trained with a small number of labeled images and a large number of unlabeled images, like a medical imaging model where only a few annotated scans are available, but the model can still leverage a large set of unlabeled scans for better generalization.

Hands-on Example: Simple Image Classification Using a Decision Tree

In this section, we'll walk through a simple example of using a decision tree for image classification. A decision tree is a simple, interpretable machine learning algorithm that splits data into subsets based on feature values, leading to a classification outcome.

Step 1: Load the dataset For this example, we'll use the **MNIST dataset**, which contains images of handwritten digits (0-9). Each image is 28x28 pixels, and the task is to classify each image as one of the digits.

```python
Copy
from sklearn.datasets import fetch_openml
import numpy as np
```

```
# Load MNIST dataset
mnist = fetch_openml('mnist_784')
X = np.array(mnist.data)
y = np.array(mnist.target)
```

Step 2: Preprocessing the data Since the decision tree algorithm doesn't require feature scaling, we'll just reshape the data to fit the algorithm's input requirements.

```python
Copy
# Normalize the pixel values
X = X / 255.0
```

Step 3: Train a Decision Tree Classifier We'll use Scikit-learn's `DecisionTreeClassifier` to train the model.

```python
Copy
from sklearn.model_selection import train_test_split
from sklearn.tree import DecisionTreeClassifier
from sklearn.metrics import accuracy_score

# Split the data into training and testing sets
```

```
X_train, X_test, y_train, y_test =
train_test_split(X, y, test_size=0.2,
random_state=42)

# Create and train the decision tree
classifier
clf                                    =
DecisionTreeClassifier(random_state=
42)
clf.fit(X_train, y_train)
```

Step 4: Make Predictions Now, we'll use the trained model to make predictions on the test set and evaluate its performance.

```python
Copy
# Make predictions on the test set
y_pred = clf.predict(X_test)

# Evaluate the model
accuracy   =   accuracy_score(y_test,
y_pred)
print(f'Accuracy: {accuracy:.4f}')
```

Output: The model will output an accuracy score, which represents how well the decision tree classifier has learned to classify the handwritten digits from the MNIST dataset.

This hands-on example demonstrates how to use a decision tree for a simple image classification task. In future chapters, we'll explore more complex and powerful models like Convolutional Neural Networks (CNNs), which are better suited for image-related tasks.

CHAPTER 4

The Basics of Neural Networks

In this chapter, we'll explore the foundations of neural networks, which form the backbone of modern machine learning and computer vision systems. We'll break down the key components of a neural network, explain how data flows through it, and dive into the process of training the network using backpropagation. Finally, we'll implement a simple neural network to classify handwritten digits from the MNIST dataset.

What is a Neural Network?

A **neural network** is a computational model inspired by the human brain. It consists of layers of nodes, or "neurons," that work together to learn patterns in data. Neural networks are used in machine learning tasks such as classification, regression, and clustering.

- **Goal**: The goal of a neural network is to learn a function that maps inputs to outputs, based on the training data it receives. It does this by adjusting the weights of connections between neurons in such a way that the output of the network closely matches the expected result.

Neural networks are often organized into three types of layers:

1. **Input layer**: Receives the input data (e.g., image pixels).

2. **Hidden layers**: Intermediate layers where computations are performed. A network can have one or more hidden layers.
3. **Output layer**: Produces the final output (e.g., class prediction, regression value).

Components of a Neural Network

1. **Neurons**
   o A neuron in a neural network is a basic unit that receives input, processes it, and passes the result to the next layer. Each neuron performs a weighted sum of its inputs and passes the result through an activation function.
   o **Example**: In an image classification task, a neuron might take pixel values as input and output a value that contributes to identifying the object in the image.
2. **Weights**
   o Weights are parameters that control the strength of the connection between neurons. Each connection between neurons has an associated weight, which determines how much influence one neuron has on another.
   o During training, the neural network learns to adjust these weights in order to minimize the error in its predictions.
   o **Example**: In a neural network, the weight of a connection between an input pixel (e.g., 0 or 255 for grayscale intensity) and a neuron in the next layer determines how

much the pixel value will influence the network's decision.

3. **Biases**
   - Biases are added to the weighted sum of inputs to allow the network to shift the activation function, enabling the model to make better predictions. Biases are similar to the intercept term in linear regression.
   - **Example**: Without a bias, the network would always be forced to make predictions that are centered around zero, limiting its capacity to learn more complex patterns.

4. **Activation Functions**
   - Activation functions introduce non-linearity to the network, enabling it to learn and model complex patterns in the data. Without activation functions, the network would be limited to learning only linear relationships.
   - **Common activation functions**:
     - **Sigmoid**: Outputs values between 0 and 1, often used in binary classification.
     - **ReLU (Rectified Linear Unit)**: Outputs values between 0 and infinity. It's widely used in deep learning because of its simplicity and efficiency.
     - **Softmax**: Converts the outputs into probabilities for classification tasks (typically used in the output

layer   for   multi-class classification).
- **Example**: In a classification network, the activation function will help decide whether an input image corresponds to one class or another.

Forward Pass and Backpropagation

1. **Forward Pass**
   - In the forward pass, input data flows through the network, layer by layer. Each neuron in a layer performs a weighted sum of its inputs, adds the bias, and then applies an activation function. The output of the last layer is the prediction of the model.
   - **Example**: In an image recognition task, the pixel values of an image pass through the input layer, are transformed in the hidden layers, and finally lead to an output layer where the class of the image (e.g., "cat" or "dog") is predicted.
2. **Backpropagation**
   - **Backpropagation** is the process of updating the weights and biases of the network after each forward pass, using the error between the predicted output and the true output. This is done through the chain rule of calculus.
   - **Steps**:

1. Calculate the error at the output (difference between predicted and actual values).
2. Compute the gradients (partial derivatives) of the error with respect to each weight and bias.
3. Adjust the weights and biases in the direction that reduces the error using an optimization technique like **gradient descent**.

   o **Real-World Example**: If the network misclassifies an image, backpropagation adjusts the weights to reduce the error, ensuring better accuracy in future predictions.

Simple Example: Building a Neural Network to Classify Handwritten Digits (MNIST Dataset)

We'll now build a simple neural network using Python and the **Keras** library to classify handwritten digits from the **MNIST dataset**.

Step 1: Import Necessary Libraries

```python
Copy
import numpy as np
import tensorflow as tf
from tensorflow.keras.models import Sequential
from tensorflow.keras.layers import Dense, Flatten
```

```
from tensorflow.keras.datasets import
mnist
from   tensorflow.keras.utils   import
to_categorical
```

Step 2: Load and Preprocess the MNIST Dataset The MNIST dataset contains 28x28 pixel images of handwritten digits (0–9). We'll normalize the data and convert the labels into categorical format.

```python
Copy
# Load the MNIST dataset
(X_train, y_train), (X_test, y_test)
= mnist.load_data()

# Normalize the pixel values to be
between 0 and 1
X_train, X_test = X_train / 255.0,
X_test / 255.0

# Convert labels to one-hot encoding
y_train = to_categorical(y_train, 10)
y_test = to_categorical(y_test, 10)
```

Step 3: Build the Neural Network Model We'll use a simple feedforward neural network with one hidden layer.

```python
Copy
# Create the model
model = Sequential([
```

40

```
    Flatten(input_shape=(28, 28)),  #
Flatten the 28x28 images into a 1D
vector
    Dense(128, activation='relu'),  #
Hidden layer with 128 neurons and ReLU
activation
    Dense(10,   activation='softmax')
# Output layer with 10 neurons (one
for each digit)
])

# Compile the model
model.compile(optimizer='adam',

loss='categorical_crossentropy',
            metrics=['accuracy'])
```

Step 4: Train the Model Now, we'll train the model on the MNIST dataset using the training data.

```python
Copy
# Train the model
model.fit(X_train, y_train, epochs=5,
batch_size=32)
```

Step 5: Evaluate the Model Finally, we'll evaluate the model's performance on the test set.

```python
Copy
# Evaluate the model on the test set
test_loss,        test_acc        =
model.evaluate(X_test, y_test)
```

```
print(f'Test                accuracy:
{test_acc:.4f}')
```

Output: After training the model, it will output the test accuracy, which indicates how well the neural network has learned to classify handwritten digits.

Summary

- **Neural networks** are a powerful tool in machine learning, used to model complex relationships in data.
- **Key components** of a neural network include neurons, weights, biases, and activation functions.
- The **forward pass** involves calculating the output by passing data through the layers of the network, while **backpropagation** updates the weights to minimize errors.
- In our hands-on example, we built a neural network that classifies handwritten digits from the MNIST dataset using Keras.

This chapter introduced the core concepts of neural networks. In the next chapters, we'll explore more advanced architectures like Convolutional Neural Networks (CNNs), which are specialized for image recognition tasks.

CHAPTER 5

Convolutional Neural Networks (CNNs) Explained

In this chapter, we will explore **Convolutional Neural Networks (CNNs)**, a type of deep learning model that has revolutionized the field of image recognition. CNNs are particularly powerful for tasks such as image classification, object detection, and facial recognition due to their ability to automatically learn and extract hierarchical features from images.

Why CNNs are Important for Image Recognition

1. **Specialization in Image Data**
   o Traditional neural networks (fully connected networks) are designed to work with one-dimensional data, like tabular data. However, images are two-dimensional (with width and height), and they contain spatial hierarchies that fully connected networks cannot exploit efficiently.
   o CNNs, on the other hand, are designed specifically to handle two-dimensional data like images. They take advantage of spatial relationships in the data, making them well-suited for tasks involving image recognition and processing.
2. **Feature Extraction**

- CNNs automatically learn features such as edges, textures, and shapes from images. Unlike traditional machine learning algorithms that require manual feature extraction, CNNs can detect increasingly complex patterns in the data as the network deepens. This hierarchical feature extraction helps CNNs identify objects in an image regardless of the size, position, or orientation.
- Early layers of a CNN might learn simple features like edges and corners, while deeper layers might detect more complex structures like faces or cars.

3. **Parameter Sharing**
   - CNNs use a technique called **parameter sharing**, where the same set of weights (filters) is applied to different parts of the image. This reduces the number of parameters in the model and makes CNNs more computationally efficient. This also enables the network to generalize better to new, unseen images.

4. **Translation Invariance**
   - CNNs can recognize objects even if they appear in different positions within the image. This is possible because the convolutional layers apply the same filter across the entire image, allowing the network to detect objects regardless of their location.

Convolution Layers, Pooling Layers, and Fully Connected Layers

1. **Convolutional Layers**
   o The core component of a CNN is the **convolutional layer**, which applies filters (also known as kernels) to the input image. These filters are small matrices that scan the image in a sliding window fashion, performing an operation called **convolution**.
   o The result of this convolution operation is a **feature map** that represents the presence of specific features (e.g., edges, textures) in different parts of the image.
   o **Example**: A 3x3 filter might be used to detect edges in the image by highlighting areas with high contrast.
2. **Pooling Layers**
   o Pooling layers are used to reduce the spatial dimensions of the image (downsampling) while preserving important features. The most common type of pooling is **max pooling**, where the maximum value in a local region of the feature map is selected.
   o Pooling helps reduce the number of computations and prevents overfitting by making the model invariant to small translations in the input image.
   o **Example**: If a 2x2 pooling layer is used with a stride of 2, it will reduce the size of

the feature map by half, keeping only the most significant features.

3. **Fully Connected Layers**
   - After several convolutional and pooling layers, the feature maps are flattened into a 1D vector and passed through **fully connected layers**. These layers are similar to the ones in traditional neural networks, where each neuron is connected to every neuron in the previous layer.
   - The fully connected layers are responsible for making the final predictions based on the extracted features.
   - **Example**: In an image classification task, the output of the fully connected layer might correspond to the class probabilities, such as whether the image is a cat or a dog.

Real-World Application: Facial Recognition Technology

1. **Face Detection**
   - CNNs are widely used in facial recognition systems because they can automatically learn to recognize faces in images, regardless of lighting, angle, or other variations. The convolutional layers of the CNN learn to extract features like eyes, nose, mouth, and facial contours, which are critical for identifying individuals.

- o **Example**: Facebook's face recognition system uses CNNs to automatically detect faces in photos and suggest tags for users.

2. **DeepFace**
   - o **DeepFace**, a facial recognition system developed by Facebook, uses a deep CNN to recognize human faces with remarkable accuracy. The system can match faces across different lighting conditions, poses, and even age variations.
   - o **Example**: DeepFace is capable of identifying individuals by comparing the extracted features from the image of a face with a large database of known faces.

3. **Real-time Face Recognition**
   - o CNNs are also used in real-time facial recognition systems for security purposes, such as unlocking smartphones or monitoring surveillance cameras. These systems continuously analyze video frames to detect and recognize faces.
   - o **Example**: Apple's Face ID, used in iPhones, employs CNNs to identify users by analyzing facial features and comparing them to the stored template.

Hands-On Example: Implementing a Simple CNN in Python

Let's now implement a simple Convolutional Neural Network using **TensorFlow** and **Keras** to classify handwritten digits from the MNIST dataset.

Step 1: Import Necessary Libraries

```python
Copy
import numpy as np
import tensorflow as tf
from tensorflow.keras.models import Sequential
from tensorflow.keras.layers import Conv2D, MaxPooling2D, Flatten, Dense
from tensorflow.keras.datasets import mnist
from tensorflow.keras.utils import to_categorical
```

Step 2: Load and Preprocess the MNIST Dataset

The MNIST dataset consists of 28x28 pixel grayscale images of handwritten digits (0-9). We'll normalize the images and convert the labels to one-hot encoding.

```python
Copy
# Load the MNIST dataset
(X_train, y_train), (X_test, y_test) = mnist.load_data()

# Reshape the data to add a channel dimension (grayscale)
X_train = X_train.reshape(-1, 28, 28, 1)
X_test = X_test.reshape(-1, 28, 28, 1)

# Normalize pixel values to be between 0 and 1
```

48

```
X_train, X_test = X_train / 255.0,
X_test / 255.0

# Convert labels to one-hot encoding
y_train = to_categorical(y_train, 10)
y_test = to_categorical(y_test, 10)
```

Step 3: Build the CNN Model We'll define a simple CNN with one convolutional layer, one pooling layer, and two fully connected layers.

```python
python
Copy
# Create the model
model = Sequential([
    # Convolutional layer with 32
filters, kernel size of 3x3, ReLU
activation
    Conv2D(32, (3, 3),
activation='relu', input_shape=(28,
28, 1)),

    # Pooling layer with 2x2 max
pooling
    MaxPooling2D(pool_size=(2, 2)),

    # Flatten the feature maps into a
1D vector
    Flatten(),

    # Fully connected layer with 128
neurons and ReLU activation
    Dense(128, activation='relu'),
```

```
    # Output layer with 10 neurons
(one for each digit) and softmax
activation
    Dense(10, activation='softmax')
])

# Compile the model
model.compile(optimizer='adam',

loss='categorical_crossentropy',
           metrics=['accuracy'])
```

Step 4: Train the Model We'll train the model on the MNIST training data for 5 epochs.

```python
Copy
# Train the model
model.fit(X_train, y_train, epochs=5,
batch_size=32)
```

Step 5: Evaluate the Model Finally, we'll evaluate the model on the test set to see how well it performs on unseen data.

```python
Copy
# Evaluate the model on the test set
test_loss,        test_acc      =
model.evaluate(X_test, y_test)
print(f'Test              accuracy:
{test_acc:.4f}')
```

Output: After training, the model will output the test accuracy, which reflects how well the CNN has learned to classify handwritten digits.

Summary

- **CNNs** are a type of neural network specifically designed for image recognition tasks. They use convolutional and pooling layers to automatically learn hierarchical features from images.
- **Convolutional layers** extract features from the image, while **pooling layers** reduce the spatial dimensions and prevent overfitting.
- **Facial recognition** technology relies heavily on CNNs to detect and recognize faces in real-time or from static images.
- We built a simple CNN model in Python using **TensorFlow** to classify handwritten digits from the MNIST dataset.

With this foundation, you can move on to more complex applications of CNNs, such as object detection, segmentation, and even generative models.

CHAPTER 6

Exploring the Dataset Landscape

In this chapter, we'll dive into the landscape of datasets commonly used in computer vision, providing an understanding of how to select datasets for training models, and addressing some of the common challenges you'll face with real-world data. We'll also walk through the process of preparing a custom dataset for an object detection task, which is a core application in computer vision.

Public Datasets in Computer Vision

Many computer vision tasks, such as image classification, object detection, and segmentation, require large amounts of labeled data for training machine learning models. Thankfully, there are several well-established **public datasets** that provide rich resources for training and benchmarking models.

1. **ImageNet**
   - **Overview**: ImageNet is one of the most widely used datasets in the computer vision community. It contains millions of labeled images categorized into thousands of classes. ImageNet is often used to train deep learning models, especially in image classification tasks.
   - **Size**: Over 14 million images, organized into 21,841 categories.

- o **Applications**: Image classification, object detection, and visual recognition.
- o **Real-World Example**: ImageNet's large-scale image classification task, where models like **AlexNet** and **ResNet** were trained to classify images into 1,000 categories, has driven many breakthroughs in deep learning.

2. **COCO (Common Objects in Context)**
   - o **Overview**: COCO is a large-scale dataset focused on object detection, segmentation, and captioning. It provides rich annotations for over 80 object categories, along with segmentations and bounding boxes for training and evaluating object detection models.
   - o **Size**: 330,000 images and over 2.5 million labeled instances.
   - o **Applications**: Object detection, instance segmentation, and image captioning.
   - o **Real-World Example**: The COCO dataset has been used to train models that power applications like autonomous driving (e.g., detecting pedestrians, vehicles, and traffic signs) and real-time object recognition systems.

3. **Pascal VOC**
   - o **Overview**: The PASCAL Visual Object Classes (VOC) dataset is another popular dataset for object detection, segmentation, and classification. It includes images with annotated bounding

boxes for 20 object classes, making it a staple for training detection models.

- o **Size**: 10,000 images spanning 20 object classes.
- o **Applications**: Object detection and image segmentation.
- o **Real-World Example**: Used in academic papers and competitions, such as the PASCAL VOC challenge, to benchmark object detection and segmentation models.

4. **Open Images**
   - o **Overview**: Open Images is a large-scale dataset for image classification, object detection, and segmentation. It includes millions of labeled images with rich annotations like object bounding boxes, segmentation masks, and visual relationships.
   - o **Size**: Over 9 million images and 600 object classes.
   - o **Applications**: Object detection, instance segmentation, and image classification.
   - o **Real-World Example**: Google's object detection and labeling algorithms were trained using Open Images for applications such as automatic image tagging and visual search.

5. **ADE20K**
   - o **Overview**: ADE20K is a dataset for semantic segmentation tasks, where each pixel in an image is labeled with a class.

This dataset covers a wide range of indoor and outdoor scenes.

- o **Size**: 20,000 images, annotated with pixel-level labels for 150 object categories.
- o **Applications**: Semantic segmentation, autonomous driving, robotics.
- o **Real-World Example**: Used in autonomous driving systems to segment different parts of the environment, such as roads, vehicles, pedestrians, and traffic signs.

How to Select Datasets for Training Models

Selecting the right dataset for a model depends on several factors. Here are key considerations when choosing a dataset:

1. **Task Type**
   - o The type of task you want to solve (e.g., image classification, object detection, semantic segmentation) will determine the type of dataset you need. If your goal is to train a classifier, an image classification dataset (e.g., ImageNet) will be ideal. If you're building an object detection system, datasets like COCO or Pascal VOC would be more appropriate.
   - o **Example**: For a facial recognition project, you would need a dataset with labeled images of faces (e.g., LFW - Labeled Faces in the Wild).

2. **Dataset Size**
   o Large datasets often lead to better generalization and more robust models. However, larger datasets also require more computational resources. For simpler tasks or if you have limited resources, smaller datasets might be more suitable.
   o **Example**: If you're starting with deep learning and lack the resources for large-scale datasets, you might opt for a smaller dataset like **CIFAR-10** (60,000 32x32 color images in 10 classes).

3. **Data Quality and Labeling**
   o The quality of data and labeling is crucial. Ensure the dataset is well-labeled with high-quality annotations. For object detection, this might include bounding boxes and segmentation masks. Poorly labeled or noisy data can lead to inaccurate models.
   o **Example**: A well-labeled dataset like COCO will be more useful for training an object detection model than a dataset with inconsistent annotations.

4. **Domain Relevance**
   o The dataset should reflect the problem you're trying to solve. If you're working on an application related to medical images, look for datasets that provide labeled medical data. Domain-specific datasets will ensure that the model learns

the features that matter most for the task at hand.

- o **Example**: For medical image analysis, datasets like **ChestX-ray14** (for chest X-rays) would be more suitable than general object detection datasets.

5. **Diversity and Variability**
   - o Datasets with diverse examples (various lighting conditions, object orientations, backgrounds) help the model generalize better. A dataset that represents the full range of potential inputs that the model might encounter in the real world will lead to better performance in practical applications.
   - o **Example**: For autonomous driving, a dataset like **Cityscapes** is valuable because it includes various driving scenarios (urban, rural, different weather conditions).

Data Challenges: Imbalanced Data, Noise, and Labeling Issues

1. **Imbalanced Data**
   - o When the dataset has many more examples of one class than another, the model may become biased toward the majority class. This can be problematic, especially in tasks like object detection or medical imaging.
   - o **Solutions**:

- Use data augmentation to generate synthetic data for underrepresented classes.
- Employ techniques like **oversampling** or **undersampling** to balance the class distribution.
- Implement class weights in the loss function to penalize the model more for misclassifying the minority class.

2. **Noise in the Data**
   o Noise refers to irrelevant or erroneous information in the dataset, such as mislabeled images or blurry images. Noise can confuse the model and reduce its ability to generalize.
   o **Solutions**:
      - Use data cleaning techniques to remove noisy data (e.g., removing mislabeled images).
      - Use robust models or loss functions that are less sensitive to noise.

3. **Labeling Issues**
   o Labeling errors occur when annotations in the dataset are incorrect, incomplete, or inconsistent. This is especially common in complex tasks like object detection or segmentation.
   o **Solutions**:
      - Cross-check labels manually or use automated tools to verify them.

- If you don't have enough labeled data, consider using semi-supervised or weakly-supervised learning methods.

Real-World Example: Preparing a Custom Dataset for Object Detection

Imagine you want to build an object detection model to identify specific objects (e.g., cars, bikes, people) in street scene images. Here's how you would prepare a custom dataset:

1. **Step 1: Collecting the Data**
   - Collect images from public sources (e.g., Google Images) or take your own images. Ensure that the images cover a variety of scenarios (e.g., day/night, different angles, weather conditions).
2. **Step 2: Annotating the Images**
   - Label the objects in the images using annotation tools like **LabelImg** or **VGG Image Annotator (VIA)**. For each object, draw a bounding box around it and label it with the corresponding class (e.g., car, bike, pedestrian).
3. **Step 3: Organizing the Dataset**
   - Once the images are labeled, organize them into folders based on the class labels. For example, you might have folders for "cars", "bikes", and "pedestrians". Ensure that each image has

an associated label file (e.g., in XML or JSON format).

4. **Step 4: Data Augmentation**
   o To increase the diversity of your dataset, apply data augmentation techniques like random flipping, scaling, rotation, and translation to generate more training examples.

5. **Step 5: Splitting the Dataset**
   o Split your dataset into training, validation, and testing sets (typically 80% for training, 10% for validation, and 10% for testing).

6. **Step 6: Preprocessing**
   o Preprocess the images by resizing them to a uniform size, normalizing pixel values, and preparing them in the required format for the model (e.g., bounding boxes and corresponding labels).

Summary

- Public datasets like **ImageNet**, **COCO**, and **Pascal VOC** provide valuable resources for training computer vision models, and each dataset has its unique features and focus.
- When selecting a dataset, consider factors like task type, dataset size, quality, and relevance to the problem.
- Common data challenges include imbalanced data, noise, and labeling issues, but these can be

mitigated with techniques like data augmentation, noise reduction, and careful label validation.

- We walked through the process of preparing a custom dataset for an object detection task, including data collection, annotation, augmentation, and preprocessing.

This chapter has provided insights into datasets and how to handle common data challenges. As you move forward, you'll be able to select and prepare the right datasets for your own computer vision tasks.

CHAPTER 7

Image Classification with CNNs

In this chapter, we will walk through the process of classifying images using **Convolutional Neural Networks (CNNs)**. CNNs are highly effective for image classification tasks, as they can automatically learn spatial hierarchies of features in images. We'll explore the step-by-step process of building a CNN for image classification, dive into popular CNN architectures like **LeNet**, **AlexNet**, and **VGG**, and demonstrate how to use pre-trained models for quick and efficient image classification.

Step-by-Step Process of Classifying Images Using CNNs

1. **Step 1: Load and Preprocess the Dataset**
   - Before training a model, you need to load and preprocess the image data. Preprocessing includes tasks like resizing images, normalizing pixel values, and splitting the data into training, validation, and test sets.
   - **Example**: In an image classification task using the **CIFAR-10 dataset**, which contains 60,000 32x32 color images in 10 classes, we need to load and preprocess the data.

```python
Copy
```

```
from      tensorflow.keras.datasets
import cifar10
from        tensorflow.keras.utils
import to_categorical

# Load CIFAR-10 dataset
(X_train,    y_train),    (X_test,
y_test) = cifar10.load_data()

# Normalize pixel values to be
between 0 and 1
X_train,   X_test  =  X_train  /
255.0, X_test / 255.0

# Convert   labels   to   one-hot
encoding
y_train                          =
to_categorical(y_train, 10)
y_test  =  to_categorical(y_test,
10)
```

2. **Step 2: Build the CNN Model**
   o A basic CNN model for image classification consists of:
     - **Convolutional layers** to extract features.
     - **Pooling layers** to reduce the spatial dimensions of the feature maps.
     - **Fully connected layers** to make the final classification based on the extracted features.

- **Output layer** with a softmax activation for multi-class classification.
  o **Example**: Building a simple CNN model to classify CIFAR-10 images:

```python
Copy
from tensorflow.keras.models import Sequential
from tensorflow.keras.layers import Conv2D, MaxPooling2D, Flatten, Dense

model = Sequential([
    # First convolutional layer with 32 filters, kernel size of 3x3, ReLU activation
    Conv2D(32, (3, 3), activation='relu', input_shape=(32, 32, 3)),

    # Pooling layer with 2x2 max pooling
    MaxPooling2D(pool_size=(2, 2)),

    # Second convolutional layer with 64 filters
    Conv2D(64, (3, 3), activation='relu'),
    MaxPooling2D(pool_size=(2, 2)),
```

```python
    # Flatten the 3D feature map
to 1D vector
    Flatten(),

    # Fully connected layer with
128 neurons and ReLU activation
    Dense(128,
activation='relu'),

    #   Output   layer   with   10
neurons (one for each class) and
softmax activation
    Dense(10,
activation='softmax')
])

# Compile the model
model.compile(optimizer='adam',
loss='categorical_crossentropy',
metrics=['accuracy'])
```

3. **Step 3: Train the Model**
   o Once the model is built, we can train it
     using the training data. During training,
     the model learns to adjust the weights
     through backpropagation by minimizing
     the loss function (cross-entropy loss in
     this case).

```python
python
Copy
# Train the model
```

```
model.fit(X_train,      y_train,
epochs=10,          batch_size=64,
validation_data=(X_test,
y_test))
```

4. **Step 4: Evaluate the Model**
   o After training, evaluate the model's performance on the test set to determine how well it generalizes to new, unseen data.

```python
Copy
# Evaluate the model on the test
set
test_loss,       test_acc      =
model.evaluate(X_test, y_test)
print(f'Test           accuracy:
{test_acc:.4f}')
```

5. **Step 5: Make Predictions**
   o Finally, you can use the trained model to make predictions on new images.

```python
Copy
# Make predictions on new images
predictions                    =
model.predict(X_test)
print(predictions[0])         #
Probabilities of each class for
the first image in the test set
```

Exploring Architectures Like LeNet, AlexNet, and VGG

Several CNN architectures have been proposed over the years, each designed to improve performance on image classification tasks. Let's explore some of the most famous CNN architectures.

1. **LeNet**
   o **LeNet** is one of the earliest CNN architectures, developed by Yann LeCun for handwritten digit recognition (MNIST dataset). It consists of two convolutional layers followed by fully connected layers.
   o **Architecture**:
     ▪ Input layer: 32x32 grayscale image.
     ▪ Convolutional layer 1: 6 filters of size 5x5.
     ▪ Pooling layer 1: 2x2 average pooling.
     ▪ Convolutional layer 2: 16 filters of size 5x5.
     ▪ Pooling layer 2: 2x2 average pooling.
     ▪ Fully connected layers: Dense layers to classify the image.
   o **Real-World Use**: LeNet was used in early systems for reading ZIP codes and recognizing handwritten digits.
2. **AlexNet**
   o **AlexNet** is a deeper CNN architecture developed by Alex Krizhevsky, Ilya Sutskever, and Geoffrey Hinton. It gained

fame for winning the 2012 ImageNet competition with a significant margin. AlexNet introduced techniques like ReLU activation, dropout, and data augmentation to improve performance.

- o **Architecture**:
  - Input layer: 227x227x3 color image.
  - Convolutional layers: 5 convolutional layers with increasing depth (96, 256, 384, 384, 256 filters).
  - Pooling layers: Max pooling layers after convolutional layers.
  - Fully connected layers: 3 dense layers, including a 4096-neuron layer.
  - Output layer: 1000 classes with softmax activation.
- o **Real-World Use**: AlexNet was a breakthrough in deep learning for image classification and is used in various vision-related tasks today.

3. **VGG**
- o **VGG** is another deep CNN architecture that achieved excellent performance in the 2014 ImageNet competition. It is known for its simplicity and uniformity. VGG uses very small (3x3) convolution filters but deepens the network significantly.
- o **Architecture**:

- Input layer: 224x224x3 color image.
- Convolutional layers: 16 or 19 layers with 3x3 filters.
- Pooling layers: Max pooling after groups of convolutional layers.
- Fully connected layers: 3 dense layers, each with 4096 neurons.
- Output layer: 1000 classes with softmax activation.
  - **Real-World Use**: VGG is widely used as a feature extractor in transfer learning for tasks like object detection and facial recognition.

Real-World Example: Using Pre-Trained Models for Quick Classification

Instead of training a model from scratch, which can be time-consuming and computationally expensive, you can leverage **pre-trained models**. Pre-trained models are CNNs that have already been trained on large datasets like ImageNet. You can fine-tune these models for your specific task or use them directly for fast classification.

Step 1: Load a Pre-Trained Model

- Keras provides several pre-trained models, including **VGG16**, **ResNet50**, and **InceptionV3**. These models can be easily loaded with weights trained on ImageNet.

```python
Copy
from tensorflow.keras.applications
import VGG16
from tensorflow.keras.preprocessing
import image
from
tensorflow.keras.applications.vgg16
import preprocess_input
import numpy as np

# Load pre-trained VGG16 model +
higher level layers
base_model                         =
VGG16(weights='imagenet',
include_top=True)

# Load an image file that contains the
object to be recognized
img_path = 'path_to_image.jpg'     #
Change to your image path
img       =       image.load_img(img_path,
target_size=(224, 224))

# Convert the image to a numpy array
and preprocess it for VGG16
img_array = image.img_to_array(img)
img_array = np.expand_dims(img_array,
axis=0)
img_array                          =
preprocess_input(img_array)
```

Step 2: Predict Using the Pre-Trained Model

- Use the pre-trained model to make predictions on the image.

```python
Copy
# Predict the class probabilities for
the image
predictions                          =
base_model.predict(img_array)

# Decode the predictions to get the
top predicted class
from
tensorflow.keras.applications.vgg16
import decode_predictions
decoded_predictions                  =
decode_predictions(predictions,
top=1)[0]
print(f'Predicted              label:
{decoded_predictions[0][1]}      with
probability
{decoded_predictions[0][2]:.4f}')
```

- **Output**: The model will output the class label and the probability of the predicted class.

Summary

- **CNNs** are the go-to architecture for image classification tasks because they automatically learn spatial features from images, making them well-suited for computer vision problems.

- We walked through the step-by-step process of building a CNN, including loading data, building a model, training, and evaluating performance.
- Popular CNN architectures like **LeNet**, **AlexNet**, and **VGG** each made significant contributions to deep learning and are still widely used in various applications.
- Pre-trained models, such as **VGG16**, provide a fast way to perform image classification without the need for extensive training.

This chapter provides the tools and knowledge to build CNNs for image classification, as well as a roadmap to leverage pre-trained models for quick deployment.

CHAPTER 8

Transfer Learning in Computer Vision

In this chapter, we will explore the concept of **transfer learning**, an essential technique in computer vision that allows you to take advantage of pre-trained models to solve custom tasks. Transfer learning has become a game-changer in deep learning, enabling faster and more efficient model training, especially when there is limited data available for the task at hand.

What is Transfer Learning and Why It's Useful

Transfer learning is a machine learning technique where a model developed for a particular task is reused as the starting point for a model on a second task. In computer vision, this typically involves taking a pre-trained convolutional neural network (CNN) and fine-tuning it to perform well on a new task with limited data.

Why Transfer Learning is Useful:

1. **Reduces Training Time**: Training deep learning models, especially for complex tasks like image classification or object detection, can be computationally expensive and time-consuming. By starting with a pre-trained model, you save time because the model has already learned useful features from a large dataset (e.g., ImageNet).

2. **Improves Performance with Limited Data**: In many real-world applications, collecting a large, labeled dataset can be challenging. Transfer learning allows you to use a model that has already been trained on a large dataset and fine-tune it on a smaller dataset for your specific task.

3. **Leverages Learned Features**: Models like **VGG16**, **ResNet**, or **Inception** are trained on massive datasets and have learned to recognize general features in images (e.g., edges, textures, and simple shapes). Transfer learning allows you to reuse these learned features for new tasks, which can significantly improve model performance, especially in tasks with limited labeled data.

4. **Fewer Parameters to Train**: Transfer learning enables you to only train the last few layers of a model rather than training the entire model from scratch. This reduces the number of parameters to be optimized, which can make the model more efficient to train.

Using Pre-trained Models for Custom Tasks

The general approach to using transfer learning in computer vision involves the following steps:

1. **Load a Pre-Trained Model**: Choose a model that has been pre-trained on a large dataset, such as ImageNet, and load it. Popular models include **VGG16**, **ResNet50**, **InceptionV3**, and **MobileNet**. These models are available in libraries like **TensorFlow** and **Keras**.

2. **Remove the Top Layer**: The top layer of the pre-trained model (which is usually a fully connected layer for classification) is removed, as it was specifically trained for the classes in the original dataset. You will replace it with a new output layer suited to your custom task.

3. **Freeze the Base Layers**: The base layers (early layers) of the pre-trained model are typically frozen, meaning their weights are not updated during training. This allows the model to retain the learned features and focus on learning the new task-specific features.

4. **Fine-Tune the Model**: The final layers of the model are fine-tuned by training them on your custom dataset. If your dataset is similar to the original one, you may freeze fewer layers and fine-tune more layers.

5. **Train the Model on Your Data**: Train the modified model on your smaller, domain-specific dataset.

Hands-On Example: Fine-Tuning a Pre-Trained Model for Medical Image Classification

Let's now walk through an example of using **transfer learning** to classify medical images. We'll use the **ResNet50** model, pre-trained on ImageNet, and fine-tune it for classifying medical images (e.g., detecting pneumonia from chest X-rays).

Step 1: Import Libraries and Pre-Trained Model
python
Copy

```
import tensorflow as tf
from tensorflow.keras.models import
Sequential
from tensorflow.keras.layers import
Dense, GlobalAveragePooling2D
from tensorflow.keras.applications
import ResNet50
from
tensorflow.keras.preprocessing.image
import ImageDataGenerator
from tensorflow.keras.optimizers
import Adam
```

Step 2: Load the Pre-trained ResNet50 Model

Here, we load the **ResNet50** model, which is pre-trained on ImageNet. We exclude the top layer so we can add our own output layer for classification.

```python
Copy
# Load the ResNet50 model pre-trained
on ImageNet, excluding the top layer
base_model                    =
ResNet50(weights='imagenet',
include_top=False, input_shape=(224,
224, 3))

# Freeze the layers of the pre-trained
model
base_model.trainable = False
```

Step 3: Add Custom Layers for Medical Image Classification

After removing the top layer, we add custom layers that will be specific to our medical image classification task.

```python
Copy
# Create a new model
model = Sequential([
    base_model,  # Add the pre-trained ResNet50 model
    GlobalAveragePooling2D(),       # Global average pooling to reduce spatial dimensions
    Dense(1024, activation='relu'), # Fully connected layer with 1024 neurons
    Dense(1, activation='sigmoid')  # Output layer for binary classification (pneumonia or not)
])

# Compile the model
model.compile(optimizer=Adam(), loss='binary_crossentropy', metrics=['accuracy'])
```

Step 4: Prepare the Dataset

For medical image classification, you'll typically use a dataset of images that need to be preprocessed (resized, normalized) before training. You can use

ImageDataGenerator to load and augment the images on the fly during training.

```python
Copy
# Data augmentation to increase the
dataset size and variability
train_datagen                  =
ImageDataGenerator(rescale=1./255,  #
Normalize pixel values to [0, 1]

rotation_range=30,

width_shift_range=0.2,

height_shift_range=0.2,

shear_range=0.2,

zoom_range=0.2,

horizontal_flip=True)

# Assuming you have a directory of
images organized into subdirectories
for each class
train_generator                =
train_datagen.flow_from_directory(
    'path_to_train_data',  # Path to
your training dataset
    target_size=(224, 224),  # Resize
all images to 224x224
    batch_size=32,
```

```
    class_mode='binary'      #  Binary
classification (pneumonia or not)
)
```
Step 5: Train the Model

We'll now fine-tune the model on the medical image dataset. Since the pre-trained layers are frozen, only the new layers will be trained initially.

```
python
Copy
# Train the model
model.fit(train_generator, epochs=10,
steps_per_epoch=100)         #   Adjust
steps_per_epoch based on dataset size
```
Step 6: Fine-Tune the Model

After training the new layers, you can **unfreeze the base model** and fine-tune the model further by training all layers. This step can help improve performance, especially if your custom dataset differs significantly from ImageNet.

```
python
Copy
# Unfreeze  some  of  the  base  model
layers
base_model.trainable = True

# Compile  the  model  again  after
unfreezing layers
model.compile(optimizer=Adam(learnin
g_rate=1e-5),
```

```
loss='binary_crossentropy',
metrics=['accuracy'])

# Fine-tune the model
model.fit(train_generator, epochs=5,
steps_per_epoch=100)
```

Step 7: Evaluate the Model

Finally, you can evaluate the model on the test dataset to see how well it performs.

```python
Copy
# Evaluate the model on the test set
test_datagen            =
ImageDataGenerator(rescale=1./255)
test_generator          =
test_datagen.flow_from_directory(
    'path_to_test_data',
    target_size=(224, 224),
    batch_size=32,
    class_mode='binary'
)

test_loss,       test_acc       =
model.evaluate(test_generator)
print(f'Test              accuracy:
{test_acc:.4f}')
```

Summary

- **Transfer learning** allows you to take advantage of pre-trained models, saving time and computational resources by reusing learned features from large datasets like ImageNet.
- The process involves:
  1. **Loading a pre-trained model** (e.g., ResNet50, VGG16).
  2. **Removing the top layer** and replacing it with a custom output layer.
  3. **Freezing the base layers** and training only the new layers on your custom dataset.
  4. **Fine-tuning the model** by unfreezing some base layers if needed.
- We demonstrated fine-tuning a pre-trained ResNet50 model for a **binary medical image classification task** (e.g., detecting pneumonia from chest X-rays).

Transfer learning is a powerful tool, especially when dealing with limited data or when computational resources are constrained. It allows you to achieve high performance without the need to train a model from scratch.

CHAPTER 9

Object Detection: Detecting and Localizing Objects

In this chapter, we will explore the task of **object detection**, a crucial component of computer vision that involves not only identifying objects in images but also localizing them by drawing bounding boxes around the detected objects. We'll differentiate object classification from object detection, discuss popular algorithms for object detection, and provide a real-world example of detecting traffic signs in self-driving cars.

Difference Between Object Classification and Detection

1. **Object Classification**:
   - **Definition**: Object classification involves determining the category or class of an object in an image. The task is to identify **what** the object is.
   - **Output**: A single label is assigned to the image (or a region of the image) indicating the class (e.g., "cat", "dog", "car").
   - **Example**: In an image of a cat, the model will classify it as "cat".
2. **Object Detection**:
   - **Definition**: Object detection goes beyond classification by not only identifying **what** the object is but also determining

where it is located in the image. This involves drawing a bounding box around each detected object, along with its corresponding label.

- o **Output**: A set of bounding boxes, each with a class label and confidence score (indicating how likely the detected object belongs to that class).
- o **Example**: In an image containing a cat and a dog, the model will output two bounding boxes (one for the cat and one for the dog) with the corresponding class labels and confidence scores.

Key Differences:

- Object classification identifies what objects are present but does not locate them within the image.
- Object detection identifies both **what** and **where** the objects are in the image.

Popular Algorithms for Object Detection

Several algorithms have been developed to tackle the object detection problem. We will explore three of the most popular ones: **YOLO, SSD**, and **Faster R-CNN**.

1. **YOLO (You Only Look Once)**
   - o **Overview**: YOLO is a real-time object detection algorithm that performs both classification and localization in a single pass through the image. The key idea

behind YOLO is that it divides the image into a grid and predicts bounding boxes and class probabilities for each grid cell.

- **Advantages**:
  - Extremely fast (real-time detection).
  - Single-stage detector (end-to-end model).
- **How It Works**: YOLO divides the image into an $S \times S$ $S \times S$ grid, where each grid cell is responsible for detecting objects whose center lies within that cell. Each grid cell predicts:
  - The probability of an object being present.
  - The coordinates of the bounding box.
  - The class label of the object.
- **Real-World Use**: YOLO is commonly used in applications where speed is critical, such as **real-time surveillance** or **autonomous vehicles**.

Example YOLO Model:

```python
Copy
from tensorflow.keras.applications import YOLOv3
model = YOLOv3(weights="yolov3.weights")
```

2. SSD (Single Shot Multibox Detector)

- **Overview**: SSD is another popular real-time object detection algorithm. Unlike YOLO, which uses a fixed grid to predict bounding boxes, SSD uses multiple feature maps with different resolutions to detect objects at various scales.
- **Advantages**:
  - Fast, especially for detecting small objects.
  - More accurate than YOLO in some scenarios, especially for smaller objects.
- **How It Works**: SSD generates a set of default bounding boxes (called priors) at multiple locations and aspect ratios, and then adjusts these priors to match the objects in the image. It uses a convolutional network to predict the class of each object and refine the bounding box locations.
- **Real-World Use**: SSD is used in applications like **face detection**, **vehicle tracking**, and **robotics** where both speed and accuracy are important.

Example SSD Model:

```python
Copy
from
tensorflow.keras.applications
import SSD
```

```
model                              =
SSD(weights="ssd_weights.h5")
```

3. **Faster R-CNN (Region-based Convolutional Neural Network)**
   o **Overview**: Faster R-CNN is a two-stage object detection algorithm. The first stage generates region proposals (potential object locations) using a **Region Proposal Network (RPN)**. The second stage classifies these proposals and refines the bounding boxes.
   o **Advantages**:
     ▪ Higher accuracy, especially for complex object detection tasks.
     ▪ More robust than single-stage detectors like YOLO and SSD.
   o **How It Works**:
     ▪ **Region Proposal Network (RPN)**: The RPN generates region proposals by sliding a small window over the feature map and predicting whether the window contains an object and refining the bounding box.
     ▪ **Object Detection**: Once the region proposals are generated, the second network classifies these regions and refines the bounding boxes using **RoI pooling**.
   o **Real-World Use**: Faster R-CNN is commonly used in applications that require high accuracy and robustness,

86

such as **medical image analysis** and **security surveillance**.

Example Faster R-CNN Model:

```python
Copy
from tensorflow.keras.applications import FasterRCNN
model = FasterRCNN(weights="fasterrcnn_weights.h5")
```

Real-World Example: Detecting Traffic Signs in Self-Driving Cars

A common real-world application of object detection is in **autonomous vehicles**, where the car needs to recognize and localize traffic signs to make driving decisions.

1. **Problem Description**:
   o The task is to detect traffic signs (e.g., stop signs, speed limits) in images taken from cameras mounted on self-driving cars. Not only do we need to classify the traffic signs, but we also need to determine their location in the image using bounding boxes.
2. **Dataset**:
   o The **German Traffic Sign Recognition Benchmark (GTSRB)** dataset is commonly used for training traffic sign

detection models. It contains over 50,000 images of traffic signs across 43 different classes (e.g., speed limits, stop signs).

3. **Model Selection**:
   - o In this case, we can use a model like **YOLO**, which is fast and can run in real-time on embedded systems, such as the hardware of self-driving cars. This enables quick detection of traffic signs, a crucial feature for safe autonomous driving.

4. **Training the Model**:
   - o We first load the dataset, preprocess the images, and augment them to improve the model's generalization ability. We then use a pre-trained **YOLO** model (or other suitable detector) to detect and classify traffic signs in new images.

Steps:

2.   **Data Preprocessing**: Normalize the pixel values, resize images, and convert them into a format that YOLO can process.

3. **Model Fine-Tuning**: Fine-tune a pre-trained YOLO model on the traffic sign dataset.

4. **Real-Time Detection**: Use the trained model to detect and localize traffic signs in video frames taken by the car's cameras.

Example Code for Real-Time Detection:

```python
Copy
import cv2
import numpy as np
from
tensorflow.keras.applications
import YOLOv3

# Load YOLO pre-trained model
model                          =
YOLOv3(weights="yolov3.weights")

# Load video feed (from self-
driving car's camera)
cap                            =
cv2.VideoCapture('car_video.mp4'
)

while cap.isOpened():
    ret, frame = cap.read()
    if not ret:
        break

    # Preprocess the frame
    processed_frame            =
preprocess_image(frame)

    # Detect traffic signs in the
frame
    predictions                =
model.predict(processed_frame)
```

```
    # Process predictions to
extract bounding boxes and labels
    bounding_boxes, labels =
process_predictions(predictions)

    # Draw bounding boxes around
detected traffic signs
    for box, label in
zip(bounding_boxes, labels):
        cv2.rectangle(frame,
box[0], box[1], (0, 255, 0), 2)
        cv2.putText(frame,
label, (box[0][0], box[0][1] -
10), cv2.FONT_HERSHEY_SIMPLEX,
1, (0, 255, 0), 2)

    # Display the processed frame
    cv2.imshow('Traffic     Sign
Detection', frame)

    if cv2.waitKey(1) & 0xFF ==
ord('q'):
        break

cap.release()
cv2.destroyAllWindows()
```

Summary

- **Object detection** not only classifies objects but also localizes them by drawing bounding boxes around them.
- We explored **YOLO**, **SSD**, and **Faster R-CNN** as the most popular algorithms for object

detection. YOLO and SSD are fast and suitable for real-time applications, while Faster R-CNN offers higher accuracy at the cost of speed.

- **Real-world example**: Detecting traffic signs in self-driving cars is an important application of object detection. Using algorithms like YOLO, traffic signs can be detected and localized in real-time, ensuring safe navigation.

In the next chapter, we'll dive deeper into **semantic segmentation**, which is another important computer vision task that segments an image into meaningful parts.

CHAPTER 10

Image Segmentation: Breaking Down Images

In this chapter, we will explore **image segmentation**, a critical computer vision task that involves partitioning an image into different segments, making it easier to analyze. Image segmentation helps computers understand the different regions of an image, making it ideal for tasks such as object detection, medical imaging, and autonomous driving.

What is Image Segmentation?

Image segmentation is the process of dividing an image into multiple segments (or regions) based on certain characteristics, such as color, intensity, or texture. The goal is to simplify the representation of an image or make it more meaningful and easier to analyze. Each segment corresponds to a different part of the image, and each segment can represent an object or a background region.

- **Why It's Important**: Image segmentation is essential for tasks that require high-level understanding of an image. For example, in medical imaging, we need to segment regions of interest (such as tumors) for diagnosis. In autonomous vehicles, segmentation helps to differentiate between the road, pedestrians, vehicles, and other objects.

Types of Image Segmentation

1. **Semantic Segmentation**
   - **Definition**: In semantic segmentation, each pixel in the image is assigned a class label (e.g., "car", "pedestrian", "background"). However, **all instances of a class** are treated as a single entity, meaning that individual objects of the same class are not distinguished.
   - **Output**: The output is a labeled map where each pixel corresponds to a specific class.
   - **Example**: In a road scene, all pixels representing cars are labeled as "car" and all pixels representing pedestrians as "pedestrian," without differentiating between individual cars or pedestrians.
2. **Instance Segmentation**
   - **Definition**: Instance segmentation not only assigns a class label to each pixel but also distinguishes between different instances of the same class. It is a combination of object detection and semantic segmentation. This means that the model can differentiate between distinct objects of the same class (e.g., two cars in the same image).
   - **Output**: The output is a labeled map where each pixel is assigned a class label and an instance ID, making it possible to separate overlapping objects of the same class.

o **Example**: In a road scene, instance segmentation can identify each individual car and pedestrian, even if they are overlapping.

Real-World Example: Segmenting Tumors in Medical Scans

Image segmentation plays a critical role in the medical field, particularly in analyzing medical scans such as **MRI** or **CT** scans. For example, when detecting tumors, it's essential to segment the tumor region from the surrounding tissues to help doctors diagnose and plan treatment.

- **Problem Description**: A medical image might contain a tumor that needs to be isolated from the healthy tissue. Semantic segmentation can be used to label the tumor region, while instance segmentation can help if there are multiple tumors in a single scan.
- **Medical Imaging**:
  o **Tumor Segmentation**: Using segmentation, we can identify the boundaries of the tumor and distinguish it from the healthy tissue in CT or MRI scans. This segmentation helps to determine the size, shape, and location of the tumor.
  o **Radiology**: Image segmentation is also applied in radiology for tasks like identifying lesions in the brain, lung nodules, and other medical conditions.

The use of segmentation can help automate diagnosis, reducing human error and speeding up the process.

Hands-On Project: Implementing Image Segmentation Using Mask R-CNN

In this section, we'll walk through a hands-on project where we'll implement image segmentation using **Mask R-CNN**. Mask R-CNN is an extension of the Faster R-CNN object detection framework, which adds a branch for predicting segmentation masks for each object detected.

Step 1: Install Required Libraries

First, we need to install the necessary libraries. Mask R-CNN requires **TensorFlow** and **Keras**.

```bash
Copy
pip install tensorflow
pip install keras
pip install mrcnn
```

Step 2: Import Necessary Libraries

Now, let's import the libraries and functions we need for the task.

```python
Copy
import os
import numpy as np
```

```
import cv2
from matplotlib import pyplot as plt
from mrcnn.config import Config
from mrcnn.model import MaskRCNN
from mrcnn import utils
```

Step 3: Load Pre-trained Mask R-CNN Model

We will use a pre-trained Mask R-CNN model that has been trained on the **COCO** dataset. This model can detect objects like people, cars, and more, and segment them from the background.

```python
Copy
# Load pre-trained Mask R-CNN model
model = MaskRCNN(mode='inference',
model_dir='./', config=Config())
model.load_weights('mask_rcnn_coco.h
5', by_name=True)
```

Step 4: Load and Preprocess an Image

For this example, let's load a sample image (could be a medical scan or a general image), resize it, and prepare it for segmentation.

```python
Copy
# Load an image
image                              =
cv2.imread('path_to_image.jpg')

# Resize the image for Mask R-CNN
```

```
image_resized   =   cv2.resize(image,
(1024, 1024))

# Convert the image to RGB for proper
processing by Mask R-CNN
image_rgb                          =
cv2.cvtColor(image_resized,
cv2.COLOR_BGR2RGB)

# Show the image
plt.imshow(image_rgb)
plt.show()
```

Step 5: Perform Image Segmentation

Once the image is prepared, we can use Mask R-CNN to detect and segment objects in the image. The detect method returns the class IDs, bounding boxes, masks, and other information about the detected objects.

```
python
Copy
# Perform segmentation on the image
results   =   model.detect([image_rgb],
verbose=1)

# Get the results for the first image
(we only have one in this case)
r = results[0]
```

Step 6: Visualize the Segmentation Masks

We can now visualize the detected masks overlaid on the original image. The r['masks'] contains the binary masks for each object detected.

```python
Copy
# Show the segmentation results
for i in range(r['masks'].shape[2]):
    mask = r['masks'][:, :, i]
    plt.imshow(mask,        cmap='jet',
alpha=0.5)
    plt.show()


# Draw the bounding boxes on the
original image
for box in r['rois']:
    cv2.rectangle(image,       (box[1],
box[0]), (box[3], box[2]), (0, 255,
0), 2)


# Display the final image with the
bounding boxes and masks
plt.imshow(image)
plt.show()
```

Step 7: Fine-Tuning the Model (Optional)

If you are working with a custom dataset, you can fine-tune Mask R-CNN on your own data (e.g., medical images) by providing it with labeled training data, such as bounding boxes and masks for tumors or lesions. This involves:

- Preparing a dataset with pixel-level masks for each object (e.g., tumor).
- Training the model using the custom dataset by defining a custom **Dataset** class and providing appropriate **configurations** for Mask R-CNN.

Step 8: Evaluating the Model

Once the model is fine-tuned on your custom data, evaluate its performance using metrics like **mean Average Precision (mAP)** and compare the predicted segmentation masks to the ground truth masks.

```python
Copy
# Evaluation on custom data
mAP      =     model.evaluate(dataset,
verbose=1)
print(f'Mean     Average     Precision:
{mAP:.4f}')
```

Summary

- **Image segmentation** is the process of partitioning an image into meaningful regions or segments. It's essential for tasks that require a high-level understanding of the image, such as medical imaging and autonomous driving.
- **Semantic segmentation** assigns a class label to each pixel, whereas **instance segmentation** not only labels each pixel but also distinguishes between different instances of the same class.
- We walked through an example of using **Mask R-CNN**, a state-of-the-art model for object detection and segmentation, to segment objects in images.
- **Real-world application**: Segmenting tumors in medical scans is a key use case of image

segmentation, allowing for automated and accurate diagnosis.

- We provided a **hands-on example** of implementing image segmentation using Mask R-CNN and visualizing the segmentation masks on images.

Image segmentation is an exciting area of computer vision with numerous practical applications. In the next chapter, we will explore **video processing** techniques and how to apply segmentation to video data.

CHAPTER 11

Image Augmentation and Data Processing

In this chapter, we will explore **image augmentation** and **data processing** techniques that are crucial for improving the performance and robustness of computer vision models. By artificially increasing the size and diversity of your training dataset, you can help your model generalize better to new, unseen data. We'll dive into common augmentation techniques and discuss their importance, followed by a real-world example of how augmentation can improve model accuracy.

Techniques for Augmenting Image Data

Image augmentation is the process of applying random transformations to images to create variations of the original data. This allows you to expose the model to different scenarios during training, which can help the model generalize better and reduce overfitting. Here are some common techniques for augmenting image data:

1. **Flipping**
   - o **Horizontal Flipping**: This is one of the most common and simple augmentation techniques. It involves flipping the image horizontally (mirroring it) to create a new variation.
   - o **Vertical Flipping**: Vertical flipping is less common but still useful in some

cases, particularly for tasks involving symmetry (e.g., medical imaging).
- o **Why It's Useful**: Flipping helps the model learn to recognize objects regardless of their orientation in the image.

Example: Flipping a picture of a cat helps the model recognize a cat both facing left and right.

2. **Rotation**
   - o **Random Rotation**: This technique rotates the image by a random degree, usually within a specified range (e.g., -30° to 30°). It introduces rotational invariance, which is important for models that need to detect objects in varying orientations.
   - o **Why It's Useful**: By applying random rotations, the model learns to identify objects from different angles, which is essential in real-world scenarios where objects may appear in various orientations.

Example: Rotating a picture of a dog allows the model to learn to recognize the dog from any angle, not just from a fixed view.

3. **Scaling and Zooming**
   - o **Random Scaling**: Scaling changes the size of the image, either by zooming in or zooming out. This technique helps the

model become invariant to changes in object size.

- o **Random Zooming**: A form of scaling, where a zooming operation is applied to randomly zoom in or out of the image, simulating objects at different distances.
- o **Why It's Useful**: Scaling ensures that the model can recognize objects whether they appear large or small in the image, simulating the effects of varying distances or camera zoom.

Example: Zooming into an image of a car allows the model to recognize the car at various distances, from close-up views to far-away views.

4. **Shifting**
   - o **Random Shifting**: Shifting involves translating (moving) the image along the X or Y axis. This is often done by a small random amount and ensures the model learns to recognize objects regardless of their position within the image.
   - o **Why It's Useful**: Shifting simulates slight camera movements or objects that appear in different parts of the image, which is common in real-world scenarios.

Example: Shifting an image of a person in the frame makes the model more robust to slight changes in the positioning of the person in the image.

5. **Shearing**
   - o **Random Shearing**: Shearing distorts the image by applying a shear transformation, where the image is slanted along a particular axis. This can simulate effects like perspective changes or tilting.
   - o **Why It's Useful**: Shearing increases the variety of transformations the model can learn, helping it recognize objects under different viewing angles or distorted perspectives.

Example: Shearing an image of a car helps the model recognize the car even if it's viewed from a slightly tilted angle.

6. **Color Variation**
   - o **Random Brightness, Contrast, and Saturation Adjustments**: Changing the brightness, contrast, and saturation of the image helps the model become invariant to lighting conditions and color variations in the environment.
   - o **Why It's Useful**: This is particularly useful in real-world applications where lighting can vary, and objects may appear under different lighting conditions (e.g., bright daylight or low-light situations).

Example: Adjusting the brightness of an image of a street scene helps the model recognize objects even in varying lighting conditions (day, night, etc.).

7. **Random Cropping**
   - **Random Crop**: Cropping involves randomly selecting a sub-region of the original image. This technique helps the model become more robust to partial occlusion and ensures that the model learns to focus on different parts of the object.
   - **Why It's Useful**: It simulates partial object occlusion, which can happen in real-world images when objects are cut off by the image frame or other objects.

Example: Cropping a picture of a car to focus on just a part of it (e.g., the car's wheels) helps the model recognize cars even when parts of the object are obscured.

Importance of Data Augmentation for Model Robustness

1. **Improves Generalization**:
   - Data augmentation increases the diversity of the training data, helping the model generalize better to unseen images. By exposing the model to different transformations of the same object, it learns to recognize the object in various situations.
2. **Reduces Overfitting**:
   - When training on a limited dataset, the model may overfit to the specific examples it has seen, memorizing them

rather than learning generalizable features. Augmentation helps reduce overfitting by artificially increasing the size of the dataset and adding variability.

3. **Simulates Real-World Variations**:
   o Data augmentation simulates real-world scenarios, such as changes in lighting, object orientation, and partial occlusion. This makes the model more robust to variations that may be encountered during actual use, such as different angles or lighting conditions.
4. **Efficient Use of Limited Data**:
   o In many cases, collecting labeled data can be expensive or time-consuming. Augmentation allows you to make the most of the available data by generating new training examples from the original dataset, helping to train a more effective model with fewer labeled examples.

Real-World Example: Using Augmentation to Improve a Model's Accuracy

Let's consider a **real-world example**: improving the accuracy of an image classification model for recognizing **dogs and cats**. You have a small dataset with limited images, and you want to augment the dataset to improve the model's performance.

Step 1: Load the Dataset and Preprocess Images
```python
Copy
```

```
from
tensorflow.keras.preprocessing.image
import ImageDataGenerator

# Initialize the ImageDataGenerator
with augmentation parameters
datagen = ImageDataGenerator(
    rescale=1./255,        # Normalize
pixel values
    rotation_range=40,       # Random
rotations
    width_shift_range=0.2,          #
Horizontal shifts
    height_shift_range=0.2,          #
Vertical shifts
    shear_range=0.2,        # Shear
transformations
    zoom_range=0.2,  # Random zooming
    horizontal_flip=True,      # Flip
images horizontally
    fill_mode='nearest'   # Fill in
missing pixels after transformations
)

# Load the dataset (assuming images
are in 'train_data' directory)
train_data                =
datagen.flow_from_directory(
    'train_data',    # Path to the
training data
    target_size=(150, 150),  # Resize
images to 150x150 pixels
    batch_size=32,
```

```
    class_mode='binary'    #  Binary
classification (dogs vs. cats)
)
```

Step 2: Train the Model with Augmented Data

Now, you can train your model using the augmented data, which helps the model generalize better to new images.

```python
Copy
from tensorflow.keras.models import
Sequential
from tensorflow.keras.layers import
Conv2D, MaxPooling2D, Flatten, Dense

# Build a simple CNN model
model = Sequential([
    Conv2D(32,          (3,          3),
activation='relu', input_shape=(150,
150, 3)),
    MaxPooling2D(2, 2),
    Conv2D(64,          (3,          3),
activation='relu'),
    MaxPooling2D(2, 2),
    Conv2D(128,          (3,          3),
activation='relu'),
    MaxPooling2D(2, 2),
    Flatten(),
    Dense(512, activation='relu'),
    Dense(1, activation='sigmoid')   #
Binary classification (dog vs cat)
])
```

```
# Compile the model
model.compile(optimizer='adam',
loss='binary_crossentropy',
metrics=['accuracy'])

# Train the model with augmented data
model.fit(train_data, epochs=10)
```

Step 3: Evaluate the Model

After training with augmented data, you can evaluate the model's performance on a validation or test set to see the improvement in accuracy.

```
python
Copy
# Evaluate the model on the test set
test_data                          =
datagen.flow_from_directory('test_da
ta',      target_size=(150,      150),
batch_size=32, class_mode='binary')
test_loss,          test_acc        =
model.evaluate(test_data)
print(f'Test                accuracy:
{test_acc:.4f}')
```

Summary

- **Image augmentation** helps to artificially increase the size and variability of the training dataset by applying random transformations such as flipping, rotation, scaling, and shifting.

- Augmentation is crucial for improving **model robustness**, reducing **overfitting**, and ensuring the model generalizes better to new, unseen data.
- By augmenting the data, the model becomes more resilient to real-world variations, such as changes in lighting, object orientation, and partial occlusion.
- We demonstrated the use of augmentation in a **dog vs. cat classification task**, showing how it can improve model performance when the dataset is limited.

CHAPTER 12

Advanced Architectures for Computer Vision

In this chapter, we will explore some of the most advanced and widely used deep learning architectures in computer vision, including **ResNet**, **Inception**, and **DenseNet**. These architectures were designed to address challenges in training deeper networks and improving performance on complex image recognition tasks. We will also discuss how deeper networks contribute to better performance and provide a real-world example of using **ResNet** for large-scale image classification.

Exploring Architectures: ResNet, Inception, DenseNet

1. **ResNet (Residual Networks)**
   - **Overview**: ResNet, introduced by **Kaiming He** and his team in 2015, is a breakthrough architecture that tackles the problem of **vanishing gradients** in very deep networks. ResNet uses **residual connections** (skip connections), where the input to a layer is passed directly to a deeper layer, allowing the network to learn the difference (residual) between the input and output.
   - **Key Concept**: The main innovation of ResNet is the **residual block**, which allows the network to be **very deep** (up to

hundreds or even thousands of layers) without suffering from degradation in performance.

- o **Architecture**: ResNet uses a stack of residual blocks, where each block includes:
  - A set of convolutional layers.
  - A skip connection that adds the input to the output of the block before passing it to the next layer.
- o **Advantages**:
  - Helps train very deep networks by alleviating the vanishing gradient problem.
  - Makes it easier to optimize deeper networks.
- o **Real-World Use**: ResNet is widely used in image classification, object detection, and many other computer vision tasks.
- o **Example**: **ResNet50** is a 50-layer deep network that balances performance and computational cost.

ResNet Architecture Example:

```python
Copy
from
tensorflow.keras.applications
import ResNet50

# Load the pre-trained ResNet50
model with weights from ImageNet
```

```
model                        =
ResNet50(weights='imagenet')
```

2. **Inception (GoogLeNet)**
   - **Overview**: Inception (also known as GoogLeNet) is an architecture introduced by **Szegedy et al.** in 2014. It was designed to optimize computational efficiency by using **parallel convolutional filters** of different sizes in a single layer. The network uses a concept called **Inception modules** to improve performance while keeping computational resources manageable.
   - **Key Concept**: The **Inception module** consists of multiple parallel convolution operations (with different filter sizes) that capture features at different scales. The outputs of these operations are concatenated, which allows the model to learn multi-scale features in a single layer.
   - **Architecture**: The original GoogLeNet (InceptionV1) consists of 22 layers, and subsequent versions (InceptionV2, V3) further optimize the architecture.
   - **Advantages**:
     - Efficient use of computational resources.
     - Ability to capture features at different scales due to multiple filter sizes.
   - **Real-World Use**: Inception models are widely used for image classification,

especially in cases where computational resources are limited.

- o **Example**: **InceptionV3** is an advanced version of the Inception architecture, often used for large-scale image classification tasks.

Inception Architecture Example:

```python
Copy
from
tensorflow.keras.applications
import InceptionV3

# Load the pre-trained
InceptionV3 model with weights
from ImageNet
model                    =
InceptionV3(weights='imagenet')
```

3. **DenseNet (Densely Connected Convolutional Networks)**
   - o **Overview**: DenseNet is another advanced architecture that aims to improve the flow of information and gradients throughout the network by using **dense connections**. Each layer in DenseNet receives input from all previous layers, making the network more efficient by reducing the number of parameters.
   - o **Key Concept**: In DenseNet, each layer receives not only the output from the

previous layer but also the outputs from all preceding layers. This creates dense connections between layers, which improves the flow of information and gradients.

- o **Architecture**: DenseNet uses **dense blocks**, where each block consists of several layers connected in a dense manner. The output from each block is passed to the next block.
- o **Advantages**:
  - Improves information flow and gradient propagation.
  - More efficient in terms of parameter usage compared to traditional networks.
  - Reduces overfitting due to the efficient use of features.
- o **Real-World Use**: DenseNet is used in a variety of image recognition tasks, especially when there is a need for better feature reuse and information flow.
- o **Example**: **DenseNet121** is a 121-layer network that provides high accuracy while being computationally efficient.

DenseNet Architecture Example:

```python
Copy
from
tensorflow.keras.applications
import DenseNet121
```

```
# Load the pre-trained
DenseNet121 model with weights
from ImageNet
model =
DenseNet121(weights='imagenet')
```

How Deeper Networks Improve Performance

1. **Capturing More Complex Features**:
   - o As the depth of a network increases, it can learn increasingly complex patterns in the data. Shallow networks can only learn basic features (e.g., edges, textures), while deeper networks can learn more abstract, high-level features that are crucial for distinguishing complex objects.
2. **Better Generalization**:
   - o Deeper networks have more capacity to learn rich representations of the data. With the right architecture and sufficient training data, deeper networks can generalize better to unseen examples, improving their performance on new tasks.
3. **Improved Gradient Flow**:
   - o Advanced architectures like **ResNet** and **DenseNet** use techniques like residual connections and dense connections to improve the flow of gradients during training. This prevents the vanishing gradient problem and allows the network

to train effectively, even with hundreds or thousands of layers.

4. **Feature Reuse and Efficiency**:
   - Networks like DenseNet reduce the number of parameters required by reusing features from earlier layers. This makes the network more efficient in terms of both computation and memory, without sacrificing performance.

Real-World Example: Using ResNet for Large-Scale Image Classification

In large-scale image classification tasks, such as classifying millions of images across thousands of categories (e.g., ImageNet), **ResNet** has proven to be an effective architecture due to its depth and ability to learn from large datasets.

Let's walk through a real-world example of using **ResNet50** to classify images from the **CIFAR-10** dataset, a popular dataset used for training image classification models.

Step 1: Import Libraries and Load Dataset

```python
Copy
import numpy as np
import tensorflow as tf
from tensorflow.keras.datasets import cifar10
from tensorflow.keras.applications import ResNet50
```

COMPUTER VISION SIMPLIFIED

```
from     tensorflow.keras.preprocessing
import image
from     tensorflow.keras.utils     import
to_categorical

# Load the CIFAR-10 dataset
(X_train,  y_train),  (X_test,  y_test)
= cifar10.load_data()

# Normalize the pixel values to be
between 0 and 1
X_train,  X_test  =  X_train  /  255.0,
X_test / 255.0

# Convert   the   labels   to   one-hot
encoding
y_train = to_categorical(y_train, 10)
y_test = to_categorical(y_test, 10)
```

Step 2: Build and Compile the Model

Here, we load the **ResNet50** model, pre-trained on ImageNet, and fine-tune it for the CIFAR-10 classification task.

```
python
Copy
# Load the ResNet50 model, pre-trained
on ImageNet
base_model                          =
ResNet50(weights='imagenet',
include_top=False,    input_shape=(32,
32, 3))
```

```python
# Freeze the layers of the pre-trained
ResNet50 model
base_model.trainable = False

# Build the model by adding custom
layers on top
model = tf.keras.Sequential([
    base_model,

tf.keras.layers.GlobalAveragePooling
2D(),
    tf.keras.layers.Dense(256,
activation='relu'),
    tf.keras.layers.Dense(10,
activation='softmax')
])

# Compile the model
model.compile(optimizer='adam',
loss='categorical_crossentropy',
metrics=['accuracy'])
```

Step 3: Train the Model

We'll now train the model using the CIFAR-10 training data.

```python
python
Copy
# Train the model
model.fit(X_train,              y_train,
epochs=10,              batch_size=64,
validation_data=(X_test, y_test))
```

Step 4: Evaluate the Model

Finally, we evaluate the model's performance on the test set.

```python
Copy
# Evaluate the model on the test set
test_loss,        test_acc        =
model.evaluate(X_test, y_test)
print(f'Test                accuracy:
{test_acc:.4f}')
```

Summary

- **ResNet**, **Inception**, and **DenseNet** are advanced architectures that address challenges in training deep neural networks and have become widely used in computer vision tasks.
- **Deeper networks** improve performance by learning more complex features, enhancing generalization, and improving gradient flow.
- **ResNet** uses residual connections to enable training of very deep networks, making it ideal for large-scale image classification tasks, like those found in the **ImageNet** competition.
- We demonstrated the use of **ResNet50** for **CIFAR-10 image classification**, showing how pre-trained models can be fine-tuned for custom tasks.

CHAPTER 13

Generative Models: From Images to New Images

In this chapter, we will dive into **Generative Models**, with a focus on **Generative Adversarial Networks (GANs)**. GANs are a class of deep learning models that are designed to generate new data that is similar to the training data. We will explore the inner workings of GANs, their applications in image generation and manipulation, and walk through a real-world example of using GANs for **image super-resolution**.

What Are Generative Adversarial Networks (GANs)?

Generative Adversarial Networks (GANs), introduced by **Ian Goodfellow** and his collaborators in 2014, are a class of machine learning models that aim to generate new, synthetic data that resembles a given dataset. GANs consist of two neural networks that compete with each other in a game-theoretic setup:

1. **Generator**: The generator's job is to create fake data (e.g., images) that resemble real data as closely as possible. It takes random noise as input and transforms it into a synthetic sample.
2. **Discriminator**: The discriminator's job is to distinguish between real and fake data. It takes data samples (both real and generated) and outputs a probability indicating whether the sample is real or fake.

How GANs Work:

- The generator and discriminator are trained simultaneously in a **minimax game**:
  - The generator tries to fool the discriminator by producing better fake samples.
  - The discriminator tries to become better at distinguishing real data from fake data.
- Over time, as the generator improves and the discriminator becomes more skilled at detection, the generator produces increasingly realistic data.
- The ultimate goal is for the generator to create data that is indistinguishable from real data by the discriminator.

Loss Function:

- The training process uses a **binary cross-entropy loss** for the discriminator and the generator. The generator aims to minimize the discriminator's ability to correctly classify fake data, while the discriminator tries to maximize its ability to distinguish real from fake data.

Applications of GANs in Image Generation and Manipulation

GANs have a wide range of applications, particularly in the field of **image generation** and **manipulation**. Some notable applications include:

1. **Image Generation**
   - GANs can be used to generate entirely new images from random noise. By training on large datasets of real images, GANs can generate new images that have similar features to those in the training data. This has applications in art creation, synthetic data generation, and more.
   - **Example**: GANs can generate new faces of people who do not exist, as seen in projects like **This Person Does Not Exist**.
2. **Image Super-Resolution**
   - One of the most exciting applications of GANs is in **image super-resolution**, where low-resolution images are upscaled to high-resolution images, with added detail and clarity. GANs are particularly effective at adding realistic details to upscaled images by learning from the high-resolution versions of the images in the training data.
   - **Example**: Enhancing the resolution of medical scans, satellite images, or old photographs.
3. **Image-to-Image Translation**
   - GANs can be used for image-to-image translation tasks, where an input image is transformed into another image with different characteristics. This has applications in fields such as photo enhancement, style transfer, and image colorization.

- o **Example**: Transforming black-and-white photos into color images or turning sketches into realistic images.

4. **Image Editing and Manipulation**
   - o GANs can be used to manipulate and edit images by conditioning the generator on certain aspects (such as the position of an object) to make specific changes to the image.
   - o **Example**: Modifying the background of an image, changing the facial expressions in portrait photos, or generating new clothing styles in fashion.

5. **Inpainting and Image Completion**
   - o GANs are effective for inpainting, where missing or occluded parts of an image are reconstructed in a realistic manner. The generator learns to complete the image based on its context.
   - o **Example**: Restoring damaged images or generating missing parts of an image, like filling in missing sections of an old photograph.

Real-World Example: Image Super-Resolution Using GANs

In this example, we will use a GAN-based approach to perform **image super-resolution**, where low-resolution images are enhanced to high-resolution ones. The idea is to train a GAN to take a low-resolution image and generate a high-resolution version with more detail.

Step 1: Import Necessary Libraries

```python
Copy
import tensorflow as tf
from tensorflow.keras.models import
Model
from tensorflow.keras.layers import
Input, Dense, Conv2D, UpSampling2D,
BatchNormalization
import numpy as np
import matplotlib.pyplot as plt
from
tensorflow.keras.preprocessing.image
import load_img, img_to_array
```

Step 2: Load and Preprocess the Image

For this example, let's assume we have a dataset of low-resolution images. We will load a sample image, convert it to low resolution, and then use the GAN to upscale it.

```python
Copy
# Load a high-resolution image
img = load_img('high_res_image.jpg')
img = img_to_array(img)

# Resize to create a low-resolution
version of the image (downscale and
then upscale)
```

```
low_res_img   =   tf.image.resize(img,
(32, 32))   # Resize to 32x32 for low
resolution
low_res_img                          =
tf.image.resize(low_res_img,    (128,
128))   # Upscale back to higher
resolution
```

Step 3: Build the Super-Resolution GAN Model

We'll define a simple GAN architecture for super-resolution. This will consist of a **generator** (which takes low-resolution images and upsamples them) and a **discriminator** (which distinguishes between real high-resolution images and generated ones).

- **Generator**: The generator uses upsampling layers to create higher-resolution images.
- **Discriminator**: The discriminator tries to distinguish between real high-resolution images and fake ones generated by the generator.

```python
Copy
# Generator Model
def build_generator():
    input_layer   =   Input(shape=(32,
32, 3))   # Low resolution image input
(32x32)

    # Upsampling layers to create high
resolution
    x       =       UpSampling2D(size=(4,
4))(input_layer)   # Upscale to 128x128
```

```python
    x    =    Conv2D(64,    (3,    3),
activation='relu', padding='same')(x)
    x = BatchNormalization()(x)

    x    =    Conv2D(3,    (3,    3),
activation='sigmoid',
padding='same')(x)  # Output high-res
image
    model = Model(input_layer, x)
    return model

# Discriminator Model
def build_discriminator():
    input_layer  =  Input(shape=(128,
128, 3))   # High  resolution  image
input (128x128)

    x = Conv2D(64, (3, 3), strides=2,
padding='same')(input_layer)        #
Downsample
    x = Conv2D(128, (3, 3), strides=2,
padding='same')(x)
    x = Conv2D(256, (3, 3), strides=2,
padding='same')(x)

    x = Flatten()(x)
    x               =            Dense(1,
activation='sigmoid')(x)    #  Output
real or fake
    model = Model(input_layer, x)
    return model

# Build GAN
```

```python
generator = build_generator()
discriminator = build_discriminator()

# Compile the discriminator
discriminator.compile(optimizer='ada
m',         loss='binary_crossentropy',
metrics=['accuracy'])

# Combine generator and discriminator
for training the GAN
discriminator.trainable = False    #
Freeze the discriminator during
generator training
gan_input = Input(shape=(32, 32, 3))
x = generator(gan_input)
gan_output = discriminator(x)
gan = Model(gan_input, gan_output)

gan.compile(optimizer='adam',
loss='binary_crossentropy')
```

Step 4: Training the GAN

To train the GAN, we will alternate between training the discriminator and the generator. The generator's goal is to produce images that fool the discriminator, and the discriminator's goal is to correctly classify real versus fake images.

```python
Copy
# Define training loop
for epoch in range(epochs):
```

```
    # Train discriminator with real
and fake images
    real_images = load_real_images()
# Real high-res images from dataset
    fake_images                    =
generator.predict(low_res_images)   #
Fake high-res images from generator

    # Train discriminator

discriminator.train_on_batch(real_im
ages, np.ones(batch_size))     # Real
images: label 1

discriminator.train_on_batch(fake_im
ages, np.zeros(batch_size))    # Fake
images: label 0

    # Train generator to fool the
discriminator
    gan_input = low_res_images
    gan.train_on_batch(gan_input,
np.ones(batch_size))   # Fake images:
label 1 (to fool discriminator)
```

Step 5: Super-Resolution Using GAN

Once trained, the generator can be used to upscale low-resolution images into high-resolution versions. Here's how we use the trained model to enhance the resolution of a low-res image.

```python
Copy
```

```
# Use the trained generator to upscale
a low-resolution image
generated_image                    =
generator.predict(low_res_img)
plt.imshow(generated_image[0])      #
Display the generated high-resolution
image
plt.show()
```

Summary

- **Generative Adversarial Networks (GANs)** consist of two neural networks: the **generator** (which generates fake data) and the **discriminator** (which distinguishes real data from fake data). These networks are trained together in a competitive process.
- **Applications of GANs** include generating realistic images, image-to-image translation (e.g., turning sketches into realistic images), and **image super-resolution**, where low-resolution images are upscaled to high-resolution versions with added detail.
- We demonstrated how to use **GANs for image super-resolution**, taking low-resolution images and generating high-resolution versions with more detail.

GANs are a powerful tool for generating realistic data, and their applications continue to expand. In the next chapter, we will explore more advanced techniques in

unsupervised learning and how they are applied in computer vision tasks.

CHAPTER 14

Image Recognition for Real-Time Applications

In this chapter, we will explore the challenges and techniques associated with real-time image recognition. Real-time applications, such as object detection in video streams or facial recognition in surveillance systems, require models that can process images quickly and accurately. We will discuss the common challenges in real-time image processing, strategies for optimizing models for faster inference, and provide a real-world example of **real-time object detection** in video streams.

Challenges in Real-Time Image Processing

1. **Speed vs. Accuracy Trade-off**
   o Real-time image recognition tasks often require a balance between model accuracy and inference speed. High-accuracy models, such as deep convolutional neural networks (CNNs), tend to be computationally expensive and slow. On the other hand, fast models might sacrifice accuracy in favor of speed.
   o **Challenge**: For real-time applications, models need to be fast enough to process images in near real-time (often in

milliseconds), but they must also maintain an acceptable level of accuracy.

2. **Large Input Sizes**
   o Many real-time image recognition tasks involve processing large images or video streams. Larger images provide more detail but also require more processing power and memory to handle.
   o **Challenge**: Processing large images in real-time requires significant computational resources, which might not always be available, especially on mobile devices or edge devices with limited hardware.

3. **Hardware Limitations**
   o Real-time image recognition models need to run on diverse hardware platforms, such as GPUs, CPUs, or even specialized hardware like **FPGAs** (Field-Programmable Gate Arrays) and **TPUs** (Tensor Processing Units). Each platform has different constraints in terms of processing power, memory, and latency.
   o **Challenge**: Optimizing models to run efficiently on a variety of hardware while maintaining real-time performance can be difficult, especially on devices with limited resources, such as mobile phones or embedded systems.

4. **Frame Rate Requirements**
   o In real-time video applications, a model must process multiple frames per second (FPS) to ensure smooth video playback

and accurate recognition. Typically, real-time video applications require at least **30 FPS** for smooth performance, with some applications demanding even higher rates.

- o **Challenge**: Achieving the required frame rate with high accuracy can be difficult, especially when processing complex models on limited hardware.

5. **Latency**
   - o **Latency** refers to the delay between receiving an input (an image or video frame) and producing the output (e.g., detecting objects or making a classification). For real-time applications, low latency is crucial to ensure immediate responses.
   - o **Challenge**: Reducing the latency in a model's inference pipeline while maintaining accuracy is one of the main challenges in real-time image processing.

Optimizing Models for Faster Inference

To overcome the challenges in real-time image recognition, several strategies and techniques can be employed to optimize models for faster inference. These methods help achieve high performance in terms of speed without sacrificing too much accuracy.

1. **Model Compression**
   - o **Pruning**: Pruning involves removing weights that have little impact on the

model's predictions, reducing the overall size of the model.

- o **Quantization**: Quantization reduces the precision of the weights (e.g., using 8-bit integers instead of 32-bit floats) to decrease memory usage and speed up inference.
- o **Knowledge Distillation**: Knowledge distillation involves training a smaller model (student) to mimic the performance of a larger, more complex model (teacher). This can result in a compact model that maintains a similar level of accuracy.

Example: Pruning a large ResNet model can significantly reduce its size and increase inference speed, making it suitable for real-time applications.

2. **Efficient Architectures**
   - o **MobileNets**: MobileNets are a family of lightweight, efficient models designed specifically for mobile and edge devices. They use **depthwise separable convolutions**, which separate the convolution into two parts (depthwise and pointwise), reducing the number of parameters and computation.
   - o **YOLO (You Only Look Once)**: YOLO is a real-time object detection system designed for fast inference. YOLO divides the image into a grid and predicts

bounding boxes and class probabilities in a single pass, which makes it highly efficient for real-time applications.

- o **EfficientNet**: EfficientNet uses a compound scaling method to balance depth, width, and resolution, achieving high accuracy with fewer parameters and faster inference compared to traditional architectures.

3. **Hardware Acceleration**
   - o **GPU/TPU Acceleration**: Using a GPU (Graphics Processing Unit) or TPU (Tensor Processing Unit) can drastically speed up the training and inference times of deep learning models. These hardware accelerators are specifically designed to handle large matrix operations, which are common in neural networks.
   - o **Edge Devices**: For mobile and embedded systems, models can be optimized using tools like **TensorFlow Lite** and **CoreML**, which convert models into formats optimized for edge devices with limited resources.

4. **Batch Processing**
   - o **Batch inference**: For applications that don't require real-time processing of individual frames (such as in video analysis), processing multiple frames in a batch can help optimize performance. This allows the model to make predictions for several frames at once,

reducing the overhead of running the model on each individual frame.

5. **Early Exiting**
   - Some models, especially those used in classification tasks, can be optimized using **early exiting** strategies. In these models, certain layers can be skipped if the model is confident about the output early in the process. This reduces the time spent on unnecessary computations.

Example: An early exit classifier could stop the model early if the first few layers confidently identify an object as a "cat," without needing to process the entire network.

Real-World Example: Real-Time Object Detection in Video Streams

One common real-time image recognition task is **object detection in video streams**. This involves detecting and classifying objects (such as cars, pedestrians, or traffic signs) in each frame of a video, often in real-time (30 FPS or higher).

In this example, we will use the **YOLO** (You Only Look Once) algorithm for real-time object detection. YOLO is known for its speed and accuracy, making it a popular choice for real-time applications.

Step 1: Import Necessary Libraries

```python
Copy
```

137

```
import cv2
import numpy as np
from    tensorflow.keras.applications
import YOLOv3
```

Step 2: Load the YOLO Model

We'll load a pre-trained **YOLOv3** model that has been trained on the COCO dataset for object detection. This model can detect various objects such as people, cars, dogs, and more.

```
python
Copy
# Load the pre-trained YOLOv3 model
model                               =
YOLOv3(weights="yolov3.weights")
```

Step 3: Initialize the Video Capture

Now, we will open the video stream (from a file or camera) and process each frame for object detection.

```
python
Copy
# Open a video stream (can be from a
file or camera)
cap                                 =
cv2.VideoCapture('video_stream.mp4')
# Replace with 0 for webcam

while cap.isOpened():
    ret, frame = cap.read()
    if not ret:
        break
```

```
    # Pre-process the frame for YOLO
detection
    blob                          =
cv2.dnn.blobFromImage(frame, 0.00392,
(416,   416),   (0,  0,  0),   True,
crop=False)
    model.setInput(blob)

    # Perform the detection
    layer_outputs                 =
model.forward(layer_names)

    # Post-process and draw bounding
boxes on the frame
    for output in layer_outputs:
        for detection in output:
            # Extract bounding box
coordinates, confidence score, and
class id
            ...

            # Draw bounding boxes and
labels on the frame
            cv2.rectangle(frame, (x,
y), (x + w, y + h), (0, 255, 0), 2)
            cv2.putText(frame, label,
(x, y-10), cv2.FONT_HERSHEY_SIMPLEX,
1, (0, 255, 0), 2)

    # Display the frame with
detections
```

```
cv2.imshow('Real-Time        Object
Detection', frame)

    # Exit the loop if 'q' is pressed
    if   cv2.waitKey(1)   &   0xFF   ==
ord('q'):
        break

cap.release()
cv2.destroyAllWindows()
```

Step 4: Optimize for Real-Time Performance

To ensure smooth real-time processing, we can apply some optimizations:

- **Downsample the video frames**: Process smaller frames to increase speed, though this might reduce accuracy.
- **Use batch processing**: If the application allows, process multiple frames at once to reduce overhead.
- **Use a more efficient model**: For faster processing, you can replace YOLO with a smaller and faster model like **MobileNet** or **Tiny YOLO**.

Summary

- **Challenges in real-time image processing** include balancing speed and accuracy, handling large input sizes, optimizing for limited hardware resources, and ensuring low latency and high frame rates.

- **Optimizing models for faster inference** involves techniques like model compression, efficient architectures (such as MobileNets and YOLO), hardware acceleration (e.g., GPUs and TPUs), and batch processing.
- We demonstrated a **real-time object detection** example using **YOLO** in a video stream, highlighting the application of object detection in surveillance systems, autonomous driving, and real-time video analysis.

CHAPTER 15

Visualizing Deep Learning Models

In this chapter, we will delve into the importance and techniques of **visualizing deep learning models**, specifically **Convolutional Neural Networks (CNNs)**. Visualizing CNN layers, filters, and activations provides valuable insights into how the network processes data, helping us understand what features the model is learning and how it makes predictions. This transparency is particularly useful for debugging, improving model performance, and explaining decisions in real-world applications, such as **facial recognition**.

Importance of Visualizing CNN Layers and Filters

1. **Understanding Model Behavior**:
   o CNNs learn to extract hierarchical features from images. At lower layers, the network detects simple features like edges, textures, and colors. As we move up in the layers, the network begins to recognize more complex structures, such as objects, faces, and scenes. Visualizing the activations at different layers helps us understand what the model is learning at each stage.
   o **Why It's Important**: This understanding can guide improvements, help diagnose problems like overfitting, and provide insights into how well the network is

capturing the important features of the image.

2. **Interpreting Filters**:
   - Filters (also known as kernels) in CNNs are responsible for convolving the input image and detecting specific features. Visualizing filters can help us understand the types of patterns the network is detecting. For example, early layers might focus on detecting edges, while deeper layers might detect more complex patterns such as eyes or wheels.
   - **Why It's Important**: Understanding which features the network is focusing on can help optimize the architecture, prevent unnecessary complexity, and improve model performance.

3. **Model Transparency and Explainability**:
   - Visualizing CNN activations is a crucial step in improving the transparency of deep learning models, especially in sensitive applications like facial recognition, medical diagnosis, and autonomous driving. Understanding how a model arrives at its decision helps build trust and facilitates the detection of biases or errors.
   - **Why It's Important**: In critical applications like **facial recognition**, we want to ensure the model is focusing on the right features (e.g., facial landmarks) rather than irrelevant details (e.g., background noise).

Tools for Visualizing Feature Maps and Activations

There are several tools and techniques that can help visualize CNN layers, filters, and activations:

1. **Visualizing Filters (Weights of Convolutional Layers)**
   - The filters of the convolutional layers in CNNs can be visualized as images. These filters represent the learned features of the network. For example, early filters may resemble edge detectors or color detectors, while deeper filters capture complex textures and objects.
   - **How to Visualize**:
     - Extract the weights from the convolutional layers of the network.
     - Display the filters as images to understand what features are being learned.

   Example Code (using Keras and TensorFlow):

   ```python
   Copy
   import matplotlib.pyplot as plt
   from tensorflow.keras.models import Model
   import numpy as np

   # Load pre-trained model (e.g.,
   VGG16 or ResNet50)
   ```

```
model                      =
tf.keras.applications.VGG16(weig
hts='imagenet',
include_top=False)

# Extract the first convolutional
layer
layer_name = 'block1_conv1'  #
Change to any layer in your model
layer                      =
model.get_layer(layer_name)

# Get the weights of the first
convolutional layer (filters)
filters,        biases       =
layer.get_weights()

# Normalize the filter values to
be between 0 and 1
filters    =      (filters    -
filters.min()) / (filters.max() -
filters.min())

# Plot the first few filters
n_filters = 6  # Display 6 filters
for i in range(n_filters):
    plt.subplot(1, n_filters, i +
1)
    plt.imshow(filters[:,  :,  :,
i])
    plt.axis('off')
plt.show()
```

2. **Visualizing Feature Maps (Activations)**:

- o Feature maps represent the output of the convolutional layers after applying filters. These maps show which parts of the image are being activated by the learned features. Visualizing these activations helps us understand what the model is focusing on when processing an image.
- o **How to Visualize**:
  - Use a **model hook** or **Keras functions** to extract the feature maps after each convolutional layer.
  - Display these feature maps for specific input images to see how the activations change at different layers.

Example Code (using Keras and TensorFlow):

```python
Copy
from tensorflow.keras.models import Model

# Create a model that outputs the
feature maps for the desired
layer
layer_name = 'block1_conv2'   #
Change to any convolutional layer
in your model
intermediate_model         =
Model(inputs=model.input,
```

```
outputs=model.get_layer(layer_na
me).output)

# Get the feature maps for a
specific input image
img     =     np.expand_dims(image,
axis=0)    # image should be a
preprocessed image
feature_maps                     =
intermediate_model.predict(img)

# Plot the feature maps
n_features                       =
feature_maps.shape[-1]   # Number
of feature maps
size = feature_maps.shape[1]
for i in range(n_features):
    plt.subplot(8, 8, i + 1)
    plt.imshow(feature_maps[0,
:, :, i], cmap='viridis')
    plt.axis('off')
plt.show()
```

3. **Grad-CAM (Gradient-weighted Class Activation Mapping)**:
   o **Grad-CAM** is a technique for visualizing which regions of an image contribute most to a particular decision. It uses the gradients of the target class (output) with respect to the convolutional layers' activations to create a heatmap, highlighting important regions in the image.

- ○ **How to Visualize**:
  - ▪ Calculate the gradients of the target class with respect to the last convolutional layer's activations.
  - ▪ Generate a heatmap based on these gradients and overlay it on the original image.

Example Code (using Keras and TensorFlow):

```python
Copy
import tensorflow as tf
import numpy as np
import matplotlib.pyplot as plt
from      tensorflow.keras.models
import Model
from
tensorflow.keras.preprocessing
import image

# Load the model
model                          =
tf.keras.applications.VGG16(weig
hts='imagenet')

# Prepare the input image
img_path = 'path_to_image.jpg'  #
Change this to your image path
img   =   image.load_img(img_path,
target_size=(224, 224))
img_array                      =
image.img_to_array(img)
```

```python
img_array                    =
np.expand_dims(img_array,
axis=0)
img_array                    =
tf.keras.applications.vgg16.prep
rocess_input(img_array)

# Get the last convolutional
layer
last_conv_layer              =
model.get_layer('block5_conv3')

# Create a model to get the
gradient of the class output
w.r.t. the last conv layer
grad_model                   =
Model(inputs=model.input,
outputs=[last_conv_layer.output,
model.output])

with tf.GradientTape() as tape:
    conv_output, predictions =
grad_model(img_array)
    loss      =      predictions[:,
np.argmax(predictions[0])]

# Get the gradient of the top
predicted class with respect to
the last conv layer output
grads     =     tape.gradient(loss,
conv_output)
```

```
# Pool the gradients across all
the axes (height, width)
pooled_grads                   =
tf.reduce_mean(grads,    axis=(0,
1, 2))

# Multiply each channel in the
feature map by the corresponding
gradient
conv_output = conv_output[0]
for            i           in
range(conv_output.shape[-1]):
    conv_output[:,   :,   i]   *=
pooled_grads[i]

# Generate the heatmap
heatmap   =   np.mean(conv_output,
axis=-1)
heatmap = np.maximum(heatmap, 0)
heatmap /= np.max(heatmap)

# Display the heatmap
plt.imshow(heatmap,   cmap='jet',
alpha=0.6)
plt.show()
```

Real-World Application: Understanding Model Decisions in Facial Recognition

Facial recognition systems have become increasingly important in applications such as security, surveillance, and personal device access. Understanding how a facial recognition model makes its decisions is crucial for improving the system and ensuring fairness and transparency.

1. **Problem**:
   o In facial recognition systems, the model needs to identify specific facial features (e.g., eyes, nose, mouth) to differentiate between individuals. Visualizing which features the model is focusing on can help ensure the system is making decisions based on the right characteristics (e.g., not being biased by the background or lighting).
2. **Using Grad-CAM for Facial Recognition**:
   o Grad-CAM can be used to generate heatmaps for facial recognition models, highlighting which regions of the face are most influential in the model's decision-making process. This allows for better model interpretability and can help identify any potential biases in the system.
3. **Example**:
   o In a facial recognition model, Grad-CAM might reveal that the model focuses on the eyes and mouth when identifying faces, which is expected. If the heatmap shows that the model is relying on irrelevant features (such as the background), this could indicate a problem with the training data or the model's architecture.

Summary

- **Visualizing CNN layers and filters** provides insights into what features a model is learning, helping us understand its decision-making process.
- **Tools like Grad-CAM, feature map visualization**, and **filter visualization** are essential for interpreting and improving deep learning models, especially in critical applications like facial recognition.
- We discussed **Grad-CAM** as a method for visualizing which parts of the image contribute most to the model's prediction, and how this can be applied to **facial recognition** models for better transparency.

Understanding how deep learning models make decisions is crucial for improving their accuracy, fairness, and transparency, especially in sensitive applications.

CHAPTER 16

Face Recognition Systems

In this chapter, we will explore **face recognition systems**, focusing on how they detect and recognize faces in images or video streams. We will delve into the science behind **face detection** and **face recognition**, discuss the models commonly used for facial recognition, such as **FaceNet** and **OpenCV**, and provide a real-world example of implementing a face recognition system in Python.

The Science Behind Face Detection and Recognition

1. **Face Detection**:
   - **Face detection** refers to the process of locating human faces within an image or video stream. Unlike object detection, which focuses on detecting any object, face detection is specifically tuned to find human faces in various environments, angles, lighting conditions, and occlusions.
   - **How It Works**:
     - **Haar Cascades**: A popular traditional method for face detection, which uses machine learning to train classifiers on positive and negative images to detect faces in grayscale images.
     - **HOG (Histogram of Oriented Gradients)**: Another technique

153

used to detect faces by computing the gradient of an image and detecting edges and shapes that indicate the presence of a face.

- **Deep Learning-Based Methods**: Modern approaches like **CNNs** (Convolutional Neural Networks) have revolutionized face detection, achieving better accuracy and robustness in challenging conditions.

2. **Face Recognition**:
   - **Face recognition** goes beyond detecting faces by identifying and verifying a specific individual. This involves mapping detected faces to a unique identity based on the **features** of the face.
   - **How It Works**:
     - **Face Embeddings**: Instead of comparing raw images, modern face recognition systems convert faces into **embeddings**—vectors that represent key features of a face (such as the distance between the eyes, the shape of the nose, etc.).
     - **Matching Embeddings**: Once faces are converted to embeddings, they are compared to stored embeddings in a database to identify or verify the individual.

Face recognition tasks:

- o **Identification**: Given a face, the system tries to determine who the person is by matching the face to a known set of identities.
- o **Verification**: Given a face and a claimed identity, the system verifies whether the face matches the claimed identity.

Models Used for Facial Recognition

1. **FaceNet**:
   - o **Overview**: **FaceNet** is a deep learning model developed by **Google** for face recognition. It generates a compact embedding (a 128-dimensional vector) for each face, which can be used for both verification and identification.
   - o **How It Works**:
     - **Triplet Loss Function**: FaceNet uses a triplet loss function during training, which ensures that the embeddings of similar faces are close together in the feature space, and embeddings of dissimilar faces are far apart.
     - **Applications**: FaceNet is widely used for real-time face recognition applications, from unlocking smartphones to verifying identities in security systems.

   Example Code (using pre-trained FaceNet model):

```python
python
Copy
import cv2
import numpy as np
from    keras.models    import
load_model
from
tensorflow.keras.applications
import ResNet50

# Load pre-trained FaceNet model
model                           =
load_model('facenet_keras.h5')

# Load image and preprocess
img                             =
cv2.imread('face_image.jpg')
img = cv2.resize(img, (160, 160))
# Resize to FaceNet's input size
img = np.expand_dims(img, axis=0)
# Add batch dimension

# Predict the face embedding
embedding = model.predict(img)
print("Face         Embedding:",
embedding)
```

2. **OpenCV (Open Source Computer Vision Library)**:
   o **Overview**: **OpenCV** is a popular open-source library for computer vision tasks. It includes many pre-trained classifiers, including one for face detection using

Haar Cascades and **LBP (Local Binary Patterns)**. While OpenCV can perform face detection, it is commonly used for preprocessing tasks, such as face alignment and detection, before passing the image to a deep learning model for recognition.

o **Applications**: OpenCV is widely used for both face detection (finding faces in images or video) and as a preprocessing step in larger face recognition systems.

Example Code (Face Detection using OpenCV):

```python
Copy
import cv2

# Load pre-trained Haar Cascade
Classifier for face detection
face_cascade            =
cv2.CascadeClassifier(cv2.data.h
aarcascades             +
'haarcascade_frontalface_default
.xml')

# Load image
img                     =
cv2.imread('face_image.jpg')
gray     =      cv2.cvtColor(img,
cv2.COLOR_BGR2GRAY)
```

```
# Detect faces in the image
faces                        =
face_cascade.detectMultiScale(gr
ay,            scaleFactor=1.1,
minNeighbors=5,      minSize=(30,
30))

# Draw rectangles around faces
for (x, y, w, h) in faces:
    cv2.rectangle(img, (x, y), (x
+ w, y + h), (0, 255, 0), 2)

# Display the image with detected
faces
cv2.imshow('Face       Detection',
img)
cv2.waitKey(0)
cv2.destroyAllWindows()
```

3. **DeepFace**:
   o **Overview**: **DeepFace** is a lightweight Python library built on top of Keras that wraps several pre-trained models for face recognition, including **VGG-Face**, **Facenet**, **OpenFace**, and **DeepID**.
   o **How It Works**: DeepFace simplifies the process of performing face recognition by allowing users to quickly implement face detection, verification, and identification with minimal setup.
   o **Applications**: DeepFace is commonly used for applications like verifying identities in social media platforms,

accessing secured systems, and even in security surveillance.

Example Code (Face Recognition using DeepFace):

```python
Copy
from deepface import DeepFace

# Compare two images for face recognition
result = DeepFace.verify("img1.jpg", "img2.jpg")
print("Are these images of the same person?", result['verified'])
```

Real-World Application: Implementing a Face Recognition System in Python

Let's walk through a simple real-time **face recognition** system using **OpenCV** and **FaceNet**. This system will detect and recognize faces from a webcam feed in real-time.

Step 1: Import Libraries and Load the Models

```python
Copy
import cv2
import numpy as np
from tensorflow.keras.models import load_model
```

```python
from deepface import DeepFace

# Load FaceNet or other pre-trained
face recognition model
model                              =
load_model('facenet_keras.h5')   # Or
load DeepFace model if using DeepFace
library
```

Step 2: Initialize Webcam Feed and Face Detection

We'll use **OpenCV** to capture the video feed from the webcam and detect faces in each frame using Haar cascades.

```python
python
Copy
# Initialize webcam feed
cap = cv2.VideoCapture(0)

# Load Haar cascade for face detection
face_cascade                       =
cv2.CascadeClassifier(cv2.data.haarc
ascades                            +
'haarcascade_frontalface_default.xml
')

while True:
    # Capture frame from the webcam
    ret, frame = cap.read()

    # Convert frame to grayscale for
face detection
```

```
    gray       =       cv2.cvtColor(frame,
cv2.COLOR_BGR2GRAY)

    # Detect faces in the frame
    faces                          =
face_cascade.detectMultiScale(gray,
scaleFactor=1.1,          minNeighbors=5,
minSize=(30, 30))

    for (x, y, w, h) in faces:
        # Draw rectangle around the
face
        cv2.rectangle(frame, (x, y),
(x + w, y + h), (0, 255, 0), 2)

        # Crop the face region from
the frame
        face = frame[y:y + h, x:x + w]

        # Preprocess the face image
before feeding it to the model
(resize, normalize, etc.)
        face_resized               =
cv2.resize(face, (160, 160))
        face_array                 =
np.expand_dims(face_resized, axis=0)

        # Predict the face embedding
or identity using the model (e.g.,
FaceNet)
        embedding                  =
model.predict(face_array)
```

```
        #     Optionally,    compare
embeddings  to  recognize  the  face
(e.g.,    using    DeepFace    for
verification)
        #   For   simplicity,   this
example just displays the embeddings
as a placeholder
        cv2.putText(frame,
"Embedding: " + str(embedding[0][0]),
(x,       y       -       10),
cv2.FONT_HERSHEY_SIMPLEX,   0.5,   (0,
255, 0), 2)

    # Display the frame with bounding
boxes around detected faces
        cv2.imshow('Face       Recognition
System', frame)

    # Break  the  loop  when  'q'  is
pressed
        if  cv2.waitKey(1)  &  0xFF  ==
ord('q'):
            break

cap.release()
cv2.destroyAllWindows()
```

Step 3: Face Recognition

Once the faces are detected and the embeddings are generated, you can compare these embeddings with a database of known embeddings to identify or verify individuals.

162

```python
Copy
# Compare the embeddings to recognize
or verify a person
result = DeepFace.verify("img1.jpg",
"img2.jpg")  # Compare two images of
faces
print("Are these images of the same
person?", result['verified'])
```

Summary

- **Face detection** identifies the presence of faces in an image or video stream, while **face recognition** involves identifying or verifying individuals by comparing the features of their faces.
- **OpenCV** and **FaceNet** are two popular tools used for face detection and recognition. OpenCV is useful for detecting faces in images or video, while FaceNet and DeepFace are used for generating and comparing face embeddings.
- We demonstrated how to implement a simple **face recognition system** using **OpenCV** for face detection and **FaceNet** for face recognition.
- **Real-world applications** of face recognition systems include security, surveillance, and personal device authentication.

CHAPTER 17

Using Computer Vision in Healthcare

In this chapter, we will explore the exciting and impactful applications of **computer vision** in healthcare. Specifically, we will discuss how **image recognition** is used in **medical imaging**, how **deep learning models** help diagnose diseases, and provide a real-world example of **using CNNs (Convolutional Neural Networks)** for detecting skin cancer.

Image Recognition in Medical Imaging (X-rays, MRIs, etc.)

Medical imaging is a critical component of modern healthcare, helping doctors diagnose, monitor, and treat various medical conditions. Traditional medical imaging includes techniques like **X-rays**, **MRI (Magnetic Resonance Imaging)**, **CT (Computed Tomography)** scans, and **Ultrasound**. Computer vision, powered by deep learning, has dramatically improved the accuracy, speed, and accessibility of medical image analysis.

1. **X-rays**:
   - **How It Works**: X-ray images are used to visualize the inside of the body, particularly bones and organs, by passing X-ray radiation through the body and capturing the patterns that result.

- **Applications**: X-rays are commonly used for detecting fractures, tumors, and lung conditions like pneumonia and tuberculosis.

2. **MRI (Magnetic Resonance Imaging)**:
   - **How It Works**: MRI uses strong magnetic fields and radio waves to generate detailed images of soft tissues in the body. Unlike X-rays, MRI does not use ionizing radiation, making it a safer option for certain conditions.
   - **Applications**: MRI is used for imaging the brain, spinal cord, muscles, and joints, and is critical for diagnosing neurological diseases, cancers, and joint disorders.

3. **CT Scans**:
   - **How It Works**: CT scans combine X-rays and computer processing to create detailed cross-sectional images of the body. They are used to visualize bones, blood vessels, and soft tissues.
   - **Applications**: CT scans are widely used for detecting cancers, internal injuries, and heart conditions.

4. **Ultrasound**:
   - **How It Works**: Ultrasound uses high-frequency sound waves to create images of the inside of the body. It is non-invasive and does not require radiation.
   - **Applications**: Ultrasound is used for monitoring pregnancies, visualizing internal organs, and diagnosing heart and vascular conditions.

Deep Learning Models for Diagnosing Diseases

Deep learning models, particularly **Convolutional Neural Networks (CNNs)**, have proven highly effective in analyzing medical images. These models can be trained to recognize patterns in images, identify abnormalities, and provide predictions based on the data. In healthcare, deep learning has been applied in the following areas:

1. **Disease Diagnosis**:
   o Deep learning models can be trained to detect diseases such as pneumonia, tuberculosis, and breast cancer from X-rays and CT scans. CNNs are particularly useful for tasks like **image segmentation** (locating specific regions in the image) and **classification** (diagnosing the presence of a condition).

2. **Tumor Detection**:
   o CNNs have been successfully used to identify and classify tumors in medical images, particularly in areas like **brain tumor detection**, **breast cancer detection**, and **lung cancer diagnosis**. These models can help doctors detect tumors at earlier stages, increasing the chances of successful treatment.

3. **Segmentation**:
   o In medical imaging, segmentation refers to identifying and delineating specific structures (e.g., tumors, organs) within an image. Deep learning models can

automatically segment structures such as **brain regions in MRIs** or **lesions in skin images**.

4. **Predicting Disease Progression**:
   o Models can also be used to predict the progression of diseases based on historical image data. This helps doctors plan appropriate interventions and treatments.

5. **Image Enhancement**:
   o Deep learning can also be used to enhance medical images, for example, improving the resolution of low-quality MRI or CT scans, a task known as **image super-resolution**.

Real-World Example: Using CNNs for Detecting Skin Cancer

One of the most well-known applications of deep learning in healthcare is using **CNNs** for **skin cancer detection**. **Skin cancer** is one of the most common types of cancer worldwide, and early detection can drastically improve outcomes. By using images of skin lesions (often from dermatoscopic images), CNNs can assist dermatologists in diagnosing malignant melanomas (a type of skin cancer) or benign moles.

1. **Problem**:
   o Detecting and diagnosing skin cancer requires analyzing images of skin lesions to distinguish between malignant and benign growths. Dermatologists

traditionally use visual examination or biopsy, but these methods can be time-consuming and prone to human error.

2. **Using CNNs for Skin Cancer Detection**:
   o **Dataset**: A large dataset of labeled images (containing both benign and malignant skin lesions) is needed to train the CNN. An example dataset is the **ISIC (International Skin Imaging Collaboration)** dataset, which contains thousands of labeled dermatoscopic images of skin lesions.
   o **CNN Architecture**: A CNN is trained to classify the lesions as malignant (cancerous) or benign (non-cancerous). The model learns to extract relevant features from the images (e.g., texture, color, shape) to make its predictions.

3. **How CNNs Work for Skin Cancer Detection**:
   o **Input**: The model takes images of skin lesions as input. These images are often captured using a dermatoscope, which provides high-resolution, magnified views of the skin.
   o **Feature Extraction**: The CNN extracts features from different layers, starting with basic features like edges and textures, and moving on to more complex features like shapes and patterns that differentiate malignant growths from benign ones.
   o **Classification**: The model classifies the lesion as benign or malignant based on the

learned features, providing a diagnostic decision.

4. **Example Code: Training a CNN for Skin Cancer Detection**

Here's an example of how a CNN can be trained to detect skin cancer from images using the **Keras** library in Python:

```python
Copy
import tensorflow as tf
from tensorflow.keras.models import Sequential
from tensorflow.keras.layers import Conv2D, MaxPooling2D, Flatten, Dense
from tensorflow.keras.preprocessing.image import ImageDataGenerator

# Set up data generators for training and validation datasets
train_datagen = ImageDataGenerator(rescale=1./255,

shear_range=0.2,

zoom_range=0.2,

horizontal_flip=True)

validation_datagen = ImageDataGenerator(rescale=1./255)
```

```
train_data                           =
train_datagen.flow_from_directory('p
ath_to_train_data',

target_size=(150, 150),

batch_size=32,

class_mode='binary')

validation_data                      =
validation_datagen.flow_from_directo
ry('path_to_validation_data',

target_size=(150, 150),

batch_size=32,

class_mode='binary')

# Build a simple CNN model
model = Sequential([
    Conv2D(32,          (3,          3),
activation='relu', input_shape=(150,
150, 3)),
    MaxPooling2D(2, 2),
    Conv2D(64,          (3,          3),
activation='relu'),
    MaxPooling2D(2, 2),
    Conv2D(128,         (3,          3),
activation='relu'),
    MaxPooling2D(2, 2),
```

```
Flatten(),
Dense(512, activation='relu'),
Dense(1, activation='sigmoid') #
Output      layer      for      binary
classification (benign or malignant)
])

# Compile the model
model.compile(optimizer='adam',

loss='binary_crossentropy',
            metrics=['accuracy'])

# Train the model
model.fit(train_data,
        epochs=10,

validation_data=validation_data)

# Save the trained model
model.save('skin_cancer_model.h5')
```

5. **Evaluation and Results**:
   - After training, the model can be used to classify new skin lesions. Its performance is typically evaluated using metrics like **accuracy, precision, recall**, and **F1-score**.
   - **Real-World Use**: In practice, the model can be deployed in clinical settings, where it assists dermatologists in making quick and accurate decisions regarding skin cancer detection.

6. **Benefits of Using CNNs for Skin Cancer Detection**:
    o **Early Detection**: CNNs can identify subtle features in images that may be overlooked by the human eye, enabling earlier detection of skin cancer.
    o **Consistency**: A deep learning model provides consistent results, reducing human error and subjectivity in diagnosis.
    o **Speed**: Automated image analysis accelerates the diagnostic process, allowing dermatologists to focus on more complex cases and improve patient outcomes.

Summary

- **Computer vision** and **deep learning** have revolutionized the medical field, especially in the area of **medical imaging**. Techniques like CNNs are used to analyze X-rays, MRIs, and CT scans to detect diseases and abnormalities.
- **Face detection** and **recognition** are part of a broader trend of using computer vision for **healthcare applications**.
- **Real-world applications** of computer vision in healthcare include disease detection (e.g., **skin cancer detection** using CNNs), tumor segmentation, and image enhancement.
- We demonstrated how CNNs can be used for **skin cancer detection** from dermatoscopic images, providing a real-time diagnostic tool for dermatologists.

CHAPTER 18

Augmented Reality and Computer Vision

In this chapter, we will explore the exciting intersection of **computer vision** and **augmented reality (AR)**. AR combines the real world with virtual elements to create immersive, interactive experiences. Computer vision plays a crucial role in enabling these experiences, allowing virtual objects to interact with the real world in real time. We will discuss how computer vision powers AR, how 3D models are integrated with real-time video, and provide a **real-world example** of implementing AR in mobile apps like **Pokémon Go**.

How Computer Vision Powers AR Experiences

Augmented reality (AR) overlays digital content, such as 3D models, images, or text, onto the real world, often using devices like smartphones, tablets, or AR glasses. The role of **computer vision** in AR is to understand and interpret the real-world environment in real time so that virtual elements can be placed and interact with the physical world correctly.

1. **Tracking and Localization**:
   o Computer vision enables **tracking** and **localization**, which allows the AR system to determine the position and orientation of objects in the real world. This process

is essential for placing virtual objects in the correct spatial location.

- o **Marker-based Tracking**: Involves using predefined markers (such as QR codes or images) that the AR system recognizes to place virtual objects on top of them.
- o **Markerless Tracking**: This method uses the camera feed to track features in the environment, such as corners, edges, and textures. Markerless tracking is more flexible and doesn't require specific markers.

2. **Depth Sensing and 3D Reconstruction**:
   - o **Depth sensing** allows the AR system to understand the depth of objects in the real world. This is crucial for placing virtual objects at appropriate distances from the camera and ensuring they interact realistically with the environment.
   - o **Stereo Vision** or using **LiDAR** (Light Detection and Ranging) sensors enables depth perception, helping AR apps calculate the 3D position of objects and adjust the virtual content to match the real-world environment.

3. **Object Recognition and Segmentation**:
   - o In many AR applications, recognizing and segmenting objects in the real world is necessary for placing virtual content around or on top of them. For instance, in an AR shopping app, the system needs to recognize furniture pieces and place virtual items in realistic locations.

o **Object Detection** models (such as **YOLO** or **Faster R-CNN**) are used for recognizing objects and segmenting them from the background.

4. **Lighting and Occlusion**:

o For a realistic AR experience, virtual objects must respond to real-world lighting conditions. Computer vision can be used to estimate lighting in the real world and adjust virtual objects accordingly.

o **Occlusion** occurs when virtual objects must be hidden behind real-world objects to maintain the illusion of reality. Computer vision can detect and compute the boundaries of real objects to ensure that virtual elements are occluded correctly.

Combining 3D Models with Real-Time Video

One of the most exciting aspects of AR is the combination of **3D models** with real-time video. This involves rendering virtual objects (often 3D models) and aligning them with real-world video captured through the camera.

1. **Rendering 3D Models**:

o Once the real-world environment is understood through computer vision techniques, 3D models can be positioned, scaled, and rotated based on the camera's viewpoint. These models are often created using 3D modeling software or generated from real-world data.

- o For instance, a 3D model of a virtual chair can be rendered in an AR app, allowing users to see how it would look in their living room by placing it on the floor through their mobile device.

2. **Real-Time Rendering**:
   - o To create smooth and immersive AR experiences, 3D models must be rendered in real time. This requires powerful graphics processing and efficient algorithms to ensure the virtual objects align properly with the real world.
   - o **SLAM (Simultaneous Localization and Mapping)** is often used in AR systems to track the camera's position and orientation in real time, allowing virtual objects to be placed correctly in the environment.

3. **Interaction with 3D Models**:
   - o Users can interact with virtual objects by moving, rotating, or scaling them, or by tapping on the screen. AR apps often use **gesture recognition** (such as pinch-to-zoom or swipe gestures) or **touch inputs** to allow users to manipulate virtual content.
   - o **Physics engines** are used to simulate realistic behaviors like gravity, collisions, and movement, making interactions with virtual objects feel natural.

Real-World Example: Implementing AR in Mobile Apps (e.g., Pokémon Go)

Pokémon Go is a prime example of how **AR** can be used in a mobile app to create an engaging and interactive experience. In this game, users see and interact with virtual Pokémon that appear overlaid on the real world through their smartphone cameras.

Let's break down how AR and computer vision enable this experience:

1. **Face and Environment Detection**:
   o In **Pokémon Go**, players see Pokémon that appear in their surroundings, such as sitting on a bench or standing on the sidewalk. The game uses the camera feed to capture the environment, and computer vision is used to analyze the surroundings and find appropriate places where virtual Pokémon can be placed realistically.
   o The app uses **markerless tracking** (based on environmental features like walls, benches, or floors) to understand the real world and position Pokémon accordingly.
2. **Location-Based AR**:
   o Pokémon Go uses **GPS** data to place virtual Pokémon in real-world locations. The game can detect the player's location and update the position of the virtual Pokémon based on the player's movement.

- o The app combines **real-time video** (captured by the camera) with **location data** to render Pokémon that are situated in the correct 3D space in relation to the player's position.

3. **Interaction with Virtual Objects**:
   - o Players interact with Pokémon by tapping on the screen to catch them. This action triggers an animation of the virtual object being "caught" and disappearing from the scene, mimicking the behavior of real-world interactions.

4. **ARKit and ARCore**:
   - o **Pokémon Go** uses frameworks like **ARKit** (for iOS) and **ARCore** (for Android) to help with the **tracking** and **rendering** of virtual content. These frameworks provide tools for detecting surfaces, adjusting lighting, and rendering 3D models in real time based on the camera feed.

5. **Challenges and Optimizations**:
   - o To ensure smooth gameplay, Pokémon Go optimizes rendering and real-time processing. This involves ensuring that the AR content is not too resource-intensive, maintaining a consistent frame rate, and preventing delays in object rendering.
   - o For example, when a Pokémon is captured, the system processes the user's camera feed, aligns the Pokémon in 3D space, and renders it on top of the camera

image— all while maintaining smooth interaction in real time.

Example Code for Basic AR App (Using ARKit on iOS or ARCore on Android)

Below is an example of a simple AR app using **ARKit** on **iOS** (for demonstration purposes). This app places a virtual 3D model in the real world using the phone's camera feed.

```swift
Copy
import ARKit
import SceneKit
import UIKit

class ViewController:
UIViewController, ARSCNViewDelegate {
    @IBOutlet var sceneView:
ARSCNView!

    override func viewDidLoad() {
        super.viewDidLoad()
        sceneView.delegate = self
        let configuration =
ARWorldTrackingConfiguration()

sceneView.session.run(configuration)
    }

    // Called when an AR object is
tapped
```

```
    @IBAction     func      addObject(_
sender: UITapGestureRecognizer) {
        let      tapLocation        =
sender.location(in: sceneView)
        let      hitTestResults      =
sceneView.hitTest(tapLocation, types:
.existingPlaneUsingExtent)

        if      let      result      =
hitTestResults.first {
            add3DObject(at: result)
        }
    }

    func              add3DObject(at
hitTestResult: ARHitTestResult) {
        let scene = SCNScene(named:
"art.scnassets/3DObject.scn")!
        let       node        =
scene.rootNode.childNode(withName:
"3DObject", recursively: false)!
        node.position        =
SCNVector3(hitTestResult.worldTransf
orm.columns.3.x,

hitTestResult.worldTransform.columns
.3.y,

hitTestResult.worldTransform.columns
.3.z)

sceneView.scene.rootNode.addChildNod
e(node)
```

```
    }
}
```

In this code:

- **ARSCNView** is used to display the AR content.
- When the user taps on the screen, a 3D model is placed in the real world at the location detected by the phone's camera.
- **SceneKit** is used for 3D model rendering.

Summary

- **Computer vision** is the backbone of AR experiences, enabling real-time tracking, depth sensing, and object recognition to seamlessly integrate virtual content with the real world.
- **3D models** are combined with real-time video through techniques like **SLAM, markerless tracking**, and **depth sensing** to create immersive AR experiences.
- We explored the **real-world example** of **Pokémon Go**, demonstrating how AR uses computer vision for location-based interactions, object placement, and real-time rendering.
- By leveraging frameworks like **ARKit** and **ARCore**, developers can implement AR features in mobile apps, opening up a world of possibilities for entertainment, education, retail, and more.

In the next chapter, we will explore **advanced AR techniques** and dive deeper into **spatial mapping** and **gesture recognition** in AR applications.

CHAPTER 19

Ethical Considerations in Computer Vision

In this chapter, we will explore the ethical challenges and considerations that arise with the use of **computer vision** technologies, particularly in applications such as **facial recognition** and **surveillance**. While these technologies offer numerous benefits, including improved security and efficiency, they also raise important concerns regarding **privacy**, **bias**, and **accountability**. We will discuss the key ethical issues, examine real-world examples, and consider ways to address these challenges.

Privacy Concerns in Facial Recognition and Surveillance

1. **Invasion of Privacy**:
   - **Facial recognition** and **surveillance technologies** have the ability to track individuals without their consent, raising concerns about the invasion of personal privacy. In public spaces, facial recognition systems can scan crowds and identify individuals, potentially collecting personal data without their knowledge.
   - **Problem**: People may not be aware that their faces are being scanned, leading to concerns that their personal information could be collected and used in ways they did not consent to.

Real-World Example:

- o Many **smart cities** are incorporating facial recognition into public surveillance systems to enhance security. However, the widespread use of these technologies in public spaces can infringe on the privacy of citizens who may not have opted into such systems.
- o **Example**: Cities like **London** and **San Francisco** have faced backlash for using facial recognition technology in public spaces without proper consent from citizens.

2. **Data Storage and Usage**:
   - o **Data retention** and **usage** are also concerns. If facial recognition data is stored in large databases, it becomes vulnerable to misuse. Even if data is initially collected for security purposes, there is the risk that it could be repurposed for surveillance, marketing, or other purposes without the knowledge of the individuals involved.
   - o **Problem**: Unauthorized access or use of facial recognition data could lead to identity theft, surveillance overreach, and the creation of unnecessary databases containing personal information.

Real-World Example:

- o **China's social credit system** has raised concerns about mass surveillance and facial recognition. The government has implemented widespread monitoring of citizens, tracking their behavior and assigning social scores based on various factors, including actions caught through surveillance cameras. This has sparked ethical debates about the balance between security and individual privacy.

3. **Tracking Individuals**:
   - o **Real-time tracking** of individuals in public or private spaces can result in the creation of **detailed profiles**. With the ability to track people's movements, habits, and even their facial expressions, there is a growing concern that facial recognition systems could be used to create profiles of individuals without their consent.
   - o **Problem**: The widespread deployment of facial recognition systems could enable governments or corporations to monitor individuals continuously, leading to a **loss of anonymity** and increased potential for social control.

Real-World Example:

- o **Clearview AI**, a facial recognition company, scraped images from social media platforms to build a vast database of faces for its software. This sparked significant debate about consent, privacy, and the potential for misuse, as people were unknowingly included in the database.

Bias in AI Models and Data

1. **Algorithmic Bias**:
   o **Bias in AI models** arises when the data used to train the models is not representative of the diverse population it is intended to serve. This can result in discriminatory outcomes, where certain groups of people are unfairly treated or misidentified. In facial recognition systems, for example, biased data can lead to higher error rates for people of color, women, or other marginalized groups.
   o **Problem**: If AI models are trained on biased datasets, they may reinforce and perpetuate stereotypes, leading to discrimination and inequality in decision-making.

   Real-World Example:

   o Several studies have shown that commercial **facial recognition systems** perform poorly on people of color, particularly women. For example, a 2018 study by the **National Institute of Standards and Technology (NIST)** found that many facial recognition systems had much higher error rates for Black and Asian faces compared to white faces.

- o **Example: IBM's Watson** had been used in healthcare for tasks like diagnosing diseases, but the model showed bias in how it made predictions for different ethnic groups. The system was trained on data that did not adequately represent minority populations, leading to inaccurate and unfair outcomes.

2. **Data Collection and Representation**:
   - o **Data quality and diversity** are crucial in ensuring that AI systems are fair and unbiased. If the data used to train a model is skewed (e.g., underrepresenting certain demographics or containing biased labels), the model's predictions and behaviors will also be biased.
   - o **Problem**: If facial recognition systems are primarily trained on images of white males, they will struggle to accurately recognize or classify faces of women or people of color, leading to unfair outcomes.

Real-World Example:

- o **Amazon's Rekognition** faced backlash in 2018 when it was revealed that the system incorrectly identified members of the U.S. Congress as criminals. The algorithm showed a higher error rate when identifying people of color, raising concerns about racial bias in facial recognition technologies.

3. **Bias in Healthcare**:
   - In medical AI, biases in data can lead to inequities in healthcare, particularly for underrepresented communities. AI systems that are trained on data that predominantly represents one group (e.g., white males) may be less accurate when diagnosing or providing recommendations for other groups, such as women or racial minorities.
   - **Problem**: Biased medical AI systems could exacerbate existing health disparities and lead to unfair treatment for patients from marginalized communities.

Real-World Example:

   - **The use of AI in healthcare** has been criticized for underperforming on non-white patients. A 2019 study showed that an AI system used to assess health risks was biased against Black patients, misidentifying their healthcare needs and leading to inadequate treatment recommendations.

Real-World Examples: Ethics of AI in Law Enforcement and Surveillance

1. **Surveillance in Law Enforcement**:
   o The use of facial recognition by law enforcement agencies has raised ethical concerns about the potential for overreach and **violations of civil liberties**. While facial recognition can help catch criminals and identify suspects, it can also be used to track individuals who have committed no crimes, raising concerns about surveillance and freedom.
   o **Problem**: There is a risk that facial recognition technology could be used as a tool for mass surveillance, disproportionately targeting certain groups, such as protesters, immigrants, or racial minorities.

   Real-World Example:

   o **The use of facial recognition by law enforcement in the United States** has sparked widespread debate. Cities like **San Francisco** have banned the use of facial recognition technology by local authorities, citing concerns about privacy, discrimination, and accountability. In contrast, cities like **Detroit** have used facial recognition to track individuals in public spaces, raising concerns about civil rights abuses and the potential for abuse by authorities.

2. **Predictive Policing**:
   o Predictive policing systems use AI to analyze crime data and predict where crimes are likely to occur. These systems often rely on historical crime data, which may contain biases that disproportionately affect certain communities, particularly minority groups.
   o **Problem**: If the data used to train predictive policing models reflects historical patterns of racial profiling or over-policing, the AI system will perpetuate these biases, leading to discriminatory law enforcement practices.

   Real-World Example:

   o **PredPol**, a predictive policing software, was criticized for being biased toward certain neighborhoods with high crime rates, which often correspond to low-income and minority areas. Critics argue that the software reinforces existing biases, leading to over-policing in these communities.

3. **AI in Surveillance of Protestors and Activists**:
   o Governments and corporations have increasingly used AI-based surveillance systems to monitor protests and activism.

While these systems may help prevent violence, they also pose a risk of **criminalizing** peaceful protests and stifling free expression.

o **Problem**: The use of AI surveillance in protest settings raises concerns about the **chilling effect** on free speech and the potential for repression.

Real-World Example:

o **China's use of AI surveillance** in monitoring **pro-democracy protests in Hong Kong** raised significant concerns about privacy, freedom of expression, and the potential for authoritarian control. AI-powered cameras and facial recognition were used to identify and track protesters, leading to accusations of human rights violations and political repression.

Summary

- **Ethical considerations** in computer vision, especially in facial recognition and surveillance, center around privacy concerns, algorithmic bias, and the responsible use of technology.
- **Privacy concerns** include the unauthorized collection of personal data, the potential for mass surveillance, and the storage and misuse of facial recognition data.
- **Bias in AI** can occur when the data used to train models is not representative, leading to

191

discriminatory outcomes that disproportionately affect marginalized groups.

- **Real-world examples** such as the use of facial recognition in law enforcement, predictive policing, and surveillance of protestors highlight the importance of ethical considerations in deploying AI technologies.
- **Addressing these ethical challenges** requires transparency, accountability, and the development of fair, unbiased, and privacy-respecting AI systems.

As we move forward with AI and computer vision technologies, it is crucial to balance innovation with ethical responsibility to ensure these systems are used for the benefit of society while minimizing harm.

CHAPTER 20

Evaluating Computer Vision Models

In this chapter, we will dive into the essential tools and metrics for **evaluating computer vision models**, particularly those used in tasks like **image classification**, **object detection**, and **segmentation**. Understanding how to evaluate the performance of your models is crucial for improving them and ensuring they meet real-world requirements. We will cover key **performance metrics** (like **accuracy**, **precision**, **recall**, and **F1-score**), as well as tools like **confusion matrices** and **ROC curves**. Finally, we'll walk through a **real-world example** of how to evaluate an **object detection model**.

Performance Metrics: Accuracy, Precision, Recall, F1-Score

1. **Accuracy**:
    o **Definition**: Accuracy is the most common performance metric and represents the proportion of correct predictions (both true positives and true negatives) out of all predictions made.
    o **Formula**:
    Accuracy=True Positives+True Negatives\Total Samples\text{Accuracy} = \frac{\text{True Positives} + \text{True Negatives}}{\text{Total}

Samples}}Accuracy=Total SamplesTrue Positives+True Negatives

- o **When to Use**: Accuracy is useful when the class distribution is balanced, meaning both positive and negative classes are equally represented. However, it can be misleading when dealing with imbalanced datasets (e.g., if most of the data belongs to one class).

Example: In a dataset with 95% images of dogs and 5% images of cats, a model that always predicts "dog" would have high accuracy (95%) but would not perform well in recognizing cats.

2. **Precision**:
   - o **Definition**: Precision measures the proportion of positive predictions that are actually correct. It is particularly useful when the cost of false positives is high (e.g., when a false positive leads to unnecessary actions).
   - o **Formula**:
     Precision=True PositivesTrue Positives+ False Positives\text{Precision} = \frac{\text{True Positives}}{\text{True Positives} + \text{False Positives}}Precision=True Positives+False PositivesTrue Positives
   - o **When to Use**: Precision is important when you want to minimize false positives, such as in fraud detection or

disease detection, where predicting a false positive could have serious consequences.

3. **Recall**:
   - **Definition**: Recall (also known as **sensitivity**) measures the proportion of actual positives that are correctly identified. It is particularly useful when the cost of false negatives is high (e.g., missing a tumor in a medical scan).
   - **Formula**:
     $$\text{Recall} = \frac{\text{True Positives}}{\text{True Positives} + \text{False Negatives}}$$
   - **When to Use**: Recall is important when the objective is to capture as many true positives as possible, even at the expense of false positives.

4. **F1-Score**:
   - **Definition**: The **F1-score** is the harmonic mean of precision and recall. It provides a single metric that balances both the precision and recall, making it a good measure when you need a balance between them.
   - **Formula**:
     $$\text{F1-score} = 2 \times \frac{\text{Precision} \times \text{Recall}}{\text{Precision} + \text{Recall}}$$
     F1-

score=2×Precision+RecallPrecision×Rec all

- o **When to Use**: F1-score is particularly useful when the classes are imbalanced, and you care about both precision and recall. It helps avoid extremes where you optimize for one metric at the expense of the other.

Confusion Matrices and ROC Curves

1. **Confusion Matrix**:
   - o A **confusion matrix** is a table that visualizes the performance of a classification model by comparing the predicted labels to the true labels. It provides a breakdown of true positives, true negatives, false positives, and false negatives.
   - o The confusion matrix is essential for understanding the types of errors a model is making and helps in calculating metrics like precision, recall, and accuracy.

Example Confusion Matrix for binary classification (positive and negative classes):

	Predicted Positive	**Predicted Negative**
Actual Positive	True Positive (TP)	False Negative (FN)

	Predicted Positive	Predicted Negative
Actual Negative	False Positive (FP)	True Negative (TN)

Confusion Matrix Code Example (using Python's `sklearn`):

```python
Copy
from sklearn.metrics import confusion_matrix
import numpy as np

# Sample true labels and predicted labels
y_true = [0, 1, 1, 0, 1, 1, 0]
y_pred = [0, 0, 1, 0, 1, 1, 1]

# Generate confusion matrix
cm = confusion_matrix(y_true, y_pred)
print("Confusion Matrix:")
print(cm)
```

2. **ROC Curve (Receiver Operating Characteristic Curve)**:
   o The **ROC curve** is a graphical representation of the trade-off between the true positive rate (recall) and false positive rate across different thresholds. It

shows how well a model distinguishes between classes.

o The **AUC (Area Under the Curve)** metric summarizes the ROC curve and represents the overall ability of the model to distinguish between classes. An AUC of 1 indicates perfect performance, while an AUC of 0.5 indicates random guessing.

ROC Curve Code Example (using Python's `sklearn`):

```python
Copy
import matplotlib.pyplot as plt
from sklearn.metrics import
roc_curve, auc

# Sample true labels and
predicted probabilities
y_true = [0, 1, 1, 0, 1, 1, 0]
y_scores = [0.1, 0.9, 0.8, 0.2,
0.85, 0.95, 0.3]

# Compute ROC curve and AUC
fpr, tpr, thresholds =
roc_curve(y_true, y_scores)
roc_auc = auc(fpr, tpr)

# Plot the ROC curve
```

```
plt.plot(fpr, tpr, color='blue',
lw=2, label=f'ROC curve (AUC =
{roc_auc:.2f})')
plt.plot([0,    1],    [0,    1],
color='gray', lw=2, linestyle='-
-')
plt.xlabel('False         Positive
Rate')
plt.ylabel('True Positive Rate')
plt.title('Receiver      Operating
Characteristic (ROC)')
plt.legend(loc='lower right')
plt.show()
```

Real-World Example: Evaluating Object Detection Models

In the context of **object detection**, performance evaluation is critical to understanding how well the model identifies and localizes objects in an image. Key metrics for object detection include:

1. **Precision and Recall for Object Detection**:
   o For each detected object, the model is evaluated based on its **precision** (how many of the detected objects are correct) and **recall** (how many of the actual objects were detected). These metrics can be calculated for each class of objects (e.g., cars, pedestrians).
2. **Intersection over Union (IoU)**:
   o **IoU** is a key metric for object detection. It measures the overlap between the predicted bounding box and the ground

199

truth bounding box. IoU is defined as: IoU=Area of OverlapArea of Union\text {IoU} = \frac{\text{Area of Overlap}} {\text{Area of Union}}IoU=Area of UnionArea of Overlap

- o An IoU threshold (typically 0.5) is used to determine whether a prediction is a true positive or a false positive. If the IoU is greater than the threshold, the prediction is considered correct.

3. **Average Precision (AP) and Mean Average Precision (mAP)**:
   - o **AP** measures the precision-recall trade-off for each class. The model's performance across different IoU thresholds is calculated, and the **mean average precision (mAP)** is computed by averaging the AP scores for all classes.

Example Code for Evaluating Object Detection Model:

```python
Copy
from sklearn.metrics import precision_recall_curve
import matplotlib.pyplot as plt

# Sample true labels and predicted probabilities for object detection
```

```
y_true = [1, 0, 1, 1, 0, 1]  #
Ground truth (1 = object present,
0 = no object)
y_scores = [0.9, 0.3, 0.85, 0.7,
0.2, 0.95]  # Predicted scores
for objects

# Compute precision-recall curve
precision, recall, thresholds =
precision_recall_curve(y_true,
y_scores)

# Plot Precision-Recall curve
plt.plot(recall,        precision,
color='blue', lw=2)
plt.xlabel('Recall')
plt.ylabel('Precision')
plt.title('Precision-Recall
Curve')
plt.show()

# Calculate average precision
(AP)
ap = np.mean(precision)        #
Simplified AP calculation
print(f'Average Precision (AP):
{ap:.2f}')
```

Summary

- **Evaluating computer vision models** involves understanding how well the model performs in detecting or classifying objects, segmenting images, or making predictions.

- Key **performance metrics** include **accuracy**, **precision**, **recall**, and **F1-score**, all of which help evaluate the model's ability to make correct predictions.
- **Confusion matrices** provide a detailed breakdown of the model's performance, and **ROC curves** help visualize the trade-offs between true positive rate and false positive rate across different thresholds.
- In **object detection**, additional metrics like **Intersection over Union (IoU)** and **mean Average Precision (mAP)** are critical for evaluating how well the model detects and localizes objects in images.
- By evaluating these metrics, you can gain valuable insights into how to improve the model and deploy it effectively for real-world applications.

In the next chapter, we will discuss **model deployment** and the steps involved in putting computer vision models into production.

CHAPTER 21

Challenges in Real-World Image Recognition

In this chapter, we will explore the **real-world challenges** that impact **image recognition** systems, particularly in practical applications. While computer vision models have made significant strides in accuracy, deploying these systems in dynamic, uncontrolled environments introduces unique difficulties. These challenges include environmental factors like **lighting**, **angle**, and **occlusion**, which can significantly affect the performance of image recognition systems. We will also discuss strategies for overcoming these challenges and provide a **real-world example** of how image recognition systems can operate in **low-light conditions**.

Environmental Challenges in Image Recognition

1. **Lighting Conditions**:
   - **Problem**: Lighting plays a crucial role in how well an image recognition system can detect and classify objects. Poor lighting conditions—whether due to shadows, overexposure, or low light—can cause images to appear unclear, resulting in missed detections or incorrect predictions. For example, objects may become hard to distinguish in dimly lit

rooms, or high contrast (e.g., sunlight) might wash out details.

- o **Impact on Models**: Traditional computer vision models, especially those relying on features like color or texture, can be sensitive to lighting conditions. For example, an object that looks bright under strong lighting may appear darker or lose detail in shadowed or low-light conditions.

2. **Viewing Angles**:

- o **Problem**: The angle from which an image is captured can drastically change the appearance of an object. This is particularly challenging in real-time applications like **autonomous driving**, where objects (like pedestrians, other vehicles, and traffic signs) can appear different depending on the viewpoint.

- o **Impact on Models**: Most image recognition models perform well when the object is facing directly toward the camera but can fail when the object is viewed from an extreme angle or in a rotated position. Variability in angles can lead to low accuracy, especially in tasks like face recognition or object detection.

3. **Occlusion**:

- o **Problem**: **Occlusion** occurs when an object is partially covered or obstructed by another object, making it harder for the system to identify it. This is common in crowded environments or scenarios where objects are hidden behind other objects (e.g., a person standing behind a car).

- o **Impact on Models**: Occlusion can lead to false negatives (where an object is not detected) or incorrect classifications. For example, a pedestrian partially blocked by a car may not be recognized by a model trained on fully visible humans.

4. **Background Clutter**:
   - o **Problem**: In real-world environments, objects may be placed against complex or dynamic backgrounds, making it difficult for the model to isolate the object of interest. Background clutter, such as moving people or other objects, can distract the system from focusing on the object that needs to be recognized.
   - o **Impact on Models**: Object recognition algorithms might incorrectly classify background elements or fail to identify the target object if it blends into the surroundings.

How to Overcome These Challenges in Practical Applications

1. **Data Augmentation**:
   - o **Solution**: **Data augmentation** involves artificially expanding the training dataset by applying random transformations to the images. These transformations include changes in lighting, rotation,

scaling, and adding noise to simulate challenging real-world conditions.

- o **For Example**: Randomly changing the brightness or contrast during training can help the model become more robust to varying lighting conditions. Likewise, rotating or flipping images can help the model become more invariant to changes in viewing angles.

Example: Augmenting the training set to include images with varying lighting conditions, such as overexposed or underexposed, can help the model learn to detect objects in diverse lighting situations.

2. **Use of Specialized Sensors (e.g., Infrared, Depth Sensors)**:
   - o **Solution**: In low-light or night-time conditions, traditional cameras may struggle to capture clear images. **Infrared (IR) cameras** and **depth sensors** (such as LiDAR) can provide additional data to help the system detect objects when visible light is insufficient.
   - o **For Example**: In autonomous driving, **LiDAR** sensors use laser beams to create 3D maps of the environment, allowing the vehicle to detect obstacles in the dark or in foggy conditions, even when traditional cameras cannot perform well.
3. **Improving Robustness through Transfer Learning**:

- o **Solution**: **Transfer learning** allows models to leverage pre-trained knowledge from other tasks or datasets, improving the model's performance on limited data. Models trained on diverse datasets that include varying environmental conditions (like lighting, angle, and occlusion) can adapt to new environments more effectively.
- o **For Example**: A model trained on a large dataset of outdoor images with various lighting conditions can be fine-tuned for a specific task (like detecting pedestrians in low-light settings) to improve its robustness to these challenges.

4. **Real-Time Adaptive Systems**:
   - o **Solution**: Developing **real-time adaptive systems** that can adjust their settings dynamically based on environmental factors (like lighting or motion) is another way to overcome these challenges. For example, a camera system might adjust its exposure automatically in low-light conditions to improve image quality.
   - o **For Example**: An AR application might adjust the brightness or contrast of the video feed in real-time to ensure that virtual objects remain clearly visible, even when the lighting changes.

5. **Segmentation and Occlusion Handling**:
   - o **Solution**: **Segmentation** techniques can help isolate objects from the background

and deal with occlusion. By segmenting the object from the background and focusing on key features (like edges or contours), models can improve their ability to recognize partially hidden objects.

- o **For Example**: In medical imaging, segmentation algorithms can help detect tumors or lesions even if they are partially occluded by surrounding tissues.

6. **Multi-Modal Data Integration**:
   - o **Solution**: Combining data from multiple sources (e.g., video, LiDAR, infrared) can provide a more comprehensive understanding of the environment. This multi-modal approach allows systems to leverage the strengths of each sensor type and compensate for the limitations of others.
   - o **For Example**: In autonomous vehicles, cameras (for visual recognition) are often combined with LiDAR (for depth perception) to create a richer, more reliable understanding of the environment.

Real-World Example: Image Recognition in Low-Light Conditions

One real-world scenario where image recognition faces significant challenges is in **low-light conditions**, such as during nighttime or in poorly lit indoor environments. Many traditional computer vision algorithms struggle in these conditions due to the lack of visible features, making it difficult to detect and recognize objects reliably.

Example Problem: Autonomous Vehicles at Night

- **Challenge**: In an autonomous driving scenario, vehicles need to recognize pedestrians, traffic signs, and other vehicles during the night or in low-light environments. Without proper illumination, traditional camera systems may fail to detect objects accurately, posing a safety risk.
- **Solution**: A combination of **infrared (IR) cameras** and **LiDAR** sensors can be used to detect objects in low-light environments. The IR camera captures heat signatures, helping to identify pedestrians or animals, while LiDAR provides a 3D map of the surroundings, enabling better detection of obstacles and vehicles.
- **Data Augmentation**: In addition to using specialized sensors, the model can be trained with augmented data that includes images captured under low-light conditions, such as dimly lit streets or night-time driving footage. This enables the model to adapt to various lighting conditions and improve its accuracy in real-world applications.

Example Code for Image Enhancement in Low-Light Conditions

In low-light situations, one common approach is to use **image enhancement techniques** to improve the quality of the image before applying object detection or classification. Here's an example of **histogram equalization** to improve contrast in low-light images:

```python
Copy
import cv2
import numpy as np

# Load a low-light image
img = cv2.imread('low_light_image.jpg', cv2.IMREAD_GRAYSCALE)

# Apply histogram equalization to improve contrast
equalized_img = cv2.equalizeHist(img)

# Show the original and equalized images
cv2.imshow('Original Image', img)
cv2.imshow('Equalized Image', equalized_img)

# Wait for a key press and close windows
cv2.waitKey(0)
cv2.destroyAllWindows()
```

This simple enhancement technique improves the visibility of features in low-light images, which can aid in better recognition and detection.

Summary

- **Environmental challenges** in image recognition include varying **lighting conditions**, **viewing angles**, **occlusion**, and **background clutter**. These challenges can significantly impact the performance of computer vision models in real-world scenarios.
- **Data augmentation, specialized sensors** (like IR and LiDAR), and **multi-modal data integration** are some of the strategies that can help overcome these challenges and improve model performance in diverse environments.
- In **low-light conditions**, **image enhancement** techniques (such as histogram equalization) and the use of infrared cameras or LiDAR sensors can help improve object recognition.
- We explored a **real-world example** of how autonomous vehicles use these techniques to detect and recognize objects in low-light environments, ensuring safety and reliability.

CHAPTER 22

Working with Video Data

In this chapter, we will explore the extension of computer vision techniques from still images to video data. While image recognition focuses on detecting and classifying objects in a single frame, **video analysis** adds a temporal dimension that involves tracking objects, recognizing activities, and interpreting dynamic changes over time. We'll cover key topics such as **object tracking**, **activity recognition**, and handling **temporal data and sequences**. Finally, we will provide a **real-world example** of using these techniques in **security applications**, such as detecting suspicious activities in surveillance footage.

Extending Computer Vision to Video: Object Tracking, Activity Recognition

1. **Object Tracking**:
   - **Problem**: While object detection identifies objects in individual frames, **object tracking** involves following the movement of an object across multiple frames in a video. This is crucial for applications like **autonomous vehicles**, **surveillance**, and **human-computer interaction**.
   - **How It Works**:
     - Object tracking algorithms use the positions of objects in consecutive

frames to predict their future locations. The system needs to handle challenges such as occlusion, scale changes, and varying object speed.

- Common tracking techniques include **Kalman filters**, **mean-shift tracking**, and more advanced methods like **Deep SORT (Simple Online and Realtime Tracking)**, which combines deep learning for detection and Kalman filters for tracking.

Example:

o In a surveillance system, object tracking is used to track the movement of people or vehicles across the camera's field of view. By associating detections in consecutive frames, the system can monitor the movement of specific individuals or objects in real time.

2. **Activity Recognition**:
   o **Problem**: Activity recognition goes beyond detecting and tracking objects by interpreting the behavior or actions of individuals or groups. It involves identifying patterns or sequences of actions that lead to meaningful conclusions, such as detecting **suspicious behavior**, **fall detection**, or **gesture recognition**.

- **How It Works**:
  - Activity recognition models are often based on **sequences of frames**, which are processed using **recurrent neural networks (RNNs)**, **long short-term memory (LSTM)** networks, or **3D convolutional networks (3D CNNs)**.
  - These models analyze the temporal dependencies between frames to understand the dynamics of movements over time. For instance, recognizing a person waving their hand requires understanding the sequence of frames where the hand moves upward, pauses, and then returns to a resting position.

Example:

- In a **smart home system**, activity recognition can be used to detect when a person enters a room or performs a specific action, such as sitting down on a chair. This can trigger automatic actions, such as turning on the lights or adjusting the thermostat.

3. **Combining Object Tracking and Activity Recognition**:
   - In many real-world applications, object tracking and activity recognition are

combined to provide more comprehensive insights. For example, in a **security surveillance system**, the system not only tracks the movement of a person but also analyzes their actions (e.g., loitering, entering a restricted area) to detect potentially suspicious behavior.

Example:

- o **In autonomous driving**, object tracking and activity recognition are combined to track pedestrians and vehicles and recognize their actions (e.g., crossing the road, turning) to make real-time driving decisions.

Handling Temporal Data and Sequences

1. **Temporal Data**:
   - o Unlike still images, which are treated as independent data points, video data is **sequential** and requires models that can handle the **temporal dimension**. Each frame is dependent on the previous one, and the model needs to account for the continuity and changes over time.
   - o **Recurrent Neural Networks (RNNs)** and their advanced variants, like **Long Short-Term Memory (LSTM)** networks, are particularly well-suited for sequential data, as they can retain

information from earlier frames and use it to process later frames in the sequence.

2. **Sequence Modeling with RNNs and LSTMs**:

   o **RNNs** are neural networks designed to process sequential data. They pass information from one time step to the next, making them ideal for processing video sequences, where each frame is related to the previous and subsequent ones.

   o **LSTMs** are a type of RNN designed to address the issue of long-term dependencies. They can remember information for longer periods, making them more effective for understanding longer sequences of frames.

   Example:

   o In **action recognition**, an LSTM network can process a series of frames showing a person performing a task (like walking, running, or waving) and recognize the activity based on the temporal pattern of movements.

3. **3D Convolutional Networks (3D CNNs)**:

   o **3D CNNs** extend 2D CNNs by adding a third dimension (time) to the convolutional layers, allowing the model to learn spatial and temporal features simultaneously. These models can capture both the motion and appearance of objects in video sequences.

- o **Example**: 3D CNNs are widely used for tasks like **video classification**, where the model must understand the temporal progression of actions, such as recognizing a sequence of movements corresponding to a sport like tennis.

4. **Optical Flow**:
   - o **Optical flow** is a technique used to track the movement of objects between consecutive video frames based on the apparent motion of pixels. It helps in determining the motion patterns of objects and is often used in combination with tracking algorithms to improve the accuracy of object movement analysis.
   - o **Example**: In robotics, optical flow can help a robot understand its movement within an environment or detect the movement of people or objects in a room.

Real-World Example: Detecting Actions in Video Footage for Security Applications

A **real-world application** where both object tracking and activity recognition play a critical role is in **security surveillance**. In security applications, systems need to detect, track, and understand the actions of people or objects in real-time to identify potential threats or abnormal activities.

1. **Problem**:
   - o Surveillance systems often need to monitor large areas (e.g., public spaces,

malls, or warehouses) using video feeds from multiple cameras. Detecting specific actions (e.g., running, loitering, or someone entering a restricted area) requires real-time analysis of video footage.

2. **Solution**:
   - **Object Tracking**: The system uses tracking algorithms to identify and follow the movement of people or vehicles across multiple camera feeds, ensuring no movement goes unnoticed.
   - **Activity Recognition**: The system analyzes the temporal sequence of frames to recognize suspicious activities like unauthorized access, loitering, or aggressive behavior. For instance, if a person is detected running or approaching an area they shouldn't be in, the system can trigger an alert.

Example: In a **warehouse**, an AI-powered security system can track the movement of workers and recognize actions like "entering a restricted area" or "interacting with a specific item." If a worker is detected in an area they shouldn't be, the system immediately sends an alert to security personnel.

3. **Tools and Technologies**:
   - The system would use **object detection models** (like YOLO or Faster R-CNN) to locate people or vehicles in the frames,

and **object tracking** algorithms (like SORT or Deep SORT) to follow their movements. For activity recognition, **LSTM networks** or **3D CNNs** can be employed to understand the sequence of actions and identify suspicious behavior.

4. **Implementation**:
   - **Input**: Video footage from surveillance cameras.
   - **Process**: Object tracking and activity recognition models analyze the video frames, tracking movements and recognizing actions.
   - **Output**: Alerts or logs detailing suspicious activities or potential security breaches, with timestamps and tracked individuals or objects.

Example Code: Here's a basic example of how to implement object tracking and activity recognition in Python using **OpenCV** for video processing:

```python
Copy
import cv2
import numpy as np

# Initialize video capture
(webcam or video file)
cap                    =
cv2.VideoCapture('surveillance_v
ideo.mp4')
```

```
#   Initialize    a    background
subtractor   to   detect   moving
objects
fgbg                            =
cv2.createBackgroundSubtractorMO
G2()

while cap.isOpened():
    ret, frame = cap.read()
    if not ret:
        break

    #      Apply       background
subtraction   to   detect   moving
objects
    fgmask = fgbg.apply(frame)

    #   Find   contours   in   the
foreground mask
    contours,    _           =
cv2.findContours(fgmask,
cv2.RETR_EXTERNAL,
cv2.CHAIN_APPROX_SIMPLE)

    for contour in contours:
        if
cv2.contourArea(contour) > 1000:
# Ignore small contours
            (x,   y,   w,   h)   =
cv2.boundingRect(contour)
            # Draw bounding box
around detected object
```

```
        cv2.rectangle(frame,
(x, y), (x + w, y + h), (0, 255,
0), 2)


        # Placeholder for
action    recognition    (e.g.,
running, walking, etc.)
        cv2.putText(frame,
"Detected Action", (x, y-10),
cv2.FONT_HERSHEY_SIMPLEX, 0.9,
(255, 0, 0), 2)

    # Display the processed video
frame
    cv2.imshow('Security
Surveillance', frame)

    if cv2.waitKey(1) & 0xFF ==
ord('q'):
        break

cap.release()
cv2.destroyAllWindows()
```

In this example:

- **Background subtraction** is used to detect moving objects.
- **Bounding boxes** are drawn around detected objects, and placeholder text is used to indicate the detection of suspicious activity.

Summary

- **Video data** introduces additional complexity to image recognition due to the **temporal** nature of video, requiring models that can track objects and recognize actions over time.
- **Object tracking** follows objects across frames, while **activity recognition** identifies patterns of behavior or specific actions.
- Challenges such as **lighting, occlusion**, and **viewing angles** are exacerbated in video, requiring solutions like **data augmentation**, **LSTMs**, and **3D CNNs** for temporal processing.
- We explored a **real-world example** of **security surveillance** in which object tracking and activity recognition are used to detect suspicious behavior, illustrating the practical application of these techniques.

In the next chapter, we will discuss **scaling computer vision models** for large datasets and real-time applications.

CHAPTER 23

AI in Autonomous Vehicles

In this chapter, we will explore the role of **computer vision** in the development and operation of **autonomous vehicles**. Computer vision is at the heart of self-driving technology, enabling cars to perceive and interact with the world around them. We will cover how **sensor fusion** combines data from multiple sensors, including cameras, LiDAR, and radar, to create a comprehensive view of the environment. Finally, we will examine a **real-world example** of **autonomous navigation systems** in **Tesla cars** to understand how these technologies come together to enable self-driving.

Role of Computer Vision in Self-Driving Cars

1. **Perception System**:
    - In autonomous vehicles, **computer vision** is primarily responsible for **perception**—the ability of the car to "see" and understand its environment. The perception system analyzes images captured by cameras and other sensors to detect objects, road signs, lane markings, pedestrians, other vehicles, and obstacles. It then processes this information to make driving decisions.
    - **Camera Systems**: Cameras are used to capture high-resolution images of the car's surroundings. These images are processed by computer vision algorithms

to identify objects and features like traffic lights, pedestrians, and other vehicles. In many systems, the camera setup consists of multiple cameras providing 360-degree views around the vehicle.

2. **Object Detection**:
   - o Object detection is a critical component of computer vision for autonomous vehicles. It involves identifying and classifying objects in the environment. For example, detecting pedestrians crossing the street or identifying traffic signs helps the vehicle understand the road conditions and make appropriate decisions.
   - o **Deep learning models** such as **YOLO (You Only Look Once)** or **Faster R-CNN** are commonly used for real-time object detection in self-driving cars. These models can process video frames in real time and accurately detect and localize objects.

3. **Lane Detection and Road Markings**:
   - o Lane detection helps the vehicle stay within the lane by identifying road markings (e.g., lane dividers). Computer vision algorithms use edge detection and line segmentation techniques to identify lane boundaries and ensure the vehicle follows the correct path.
   - o **Semantic segmentation** is often used in this context, where each pixel in the image is classified to indicate whether it

belongs to the road, lane markings, or other objects.

4. **Traffic Light and Sign Recognition**:
   o Recognizing **traffic lights** and **road signs** is essential for autonomous vehicles to follow traffic rules. Computer vision models analyze the visual data from cameras to detect traffic lights, identify their states (red, green, yellow), and interpret road signs (stop, yield, speed limits).
   o **Deep learning models** trained on large datasets of road signs and traffic lights help vehicles make decisions such as stopping at a red light or adhering to speed limits.

5. **Pedestrian and Vehicle Detection**:
   o **Pedestrian detection** ensures the vehicle is aware of people walking nearby, especially at intersections or pedestrian crossings. Computer vision models use cameras to detect pedestrians and anticipate their movements, allowing the vehicle to slow down or stop if needed.
   o **Vehicle detection** is crucial for avoiding collisions with other vehicles. Autonomous vehicles use computer vision to identify other cars, trucks, and motorcycles and maintain a safe distance from them.

Sensor Fusion: Combining Images, LiDAR, and Radar Data

While computer vision from cameras plays a significant role in autonomous vehicles, it is not sufficient on its own. To create a more reliable and accurate perception system, autonomous vehicles rely on **sensor fusion**, the process of combining data from multiple sensors, including cameras, **LiDAR (Light Detection and Ranging)**, and **radar**.

1. **Cameras**:
   o Cameras provide high-resolution, color images, making them ideal for recognizing objects, reading road signs, detecting traffic lights, and understanding road markings.
   o **Limitations**: Cameras are affected by lighting conditions, such as glare, shadows, and low light, and may struggle with detecting objects in poor visibility conditions (e.g., fog or rain).
2. **LiDAR**:
   o **LiDAR** uses laser light to create 3D maps of the environment. It emits laser beams and measures the time it takes for the light to return, creating a point cloud that represents the shape of objects and surfaces around the vehicle.
   o **Advantages**: LiDAR provides highly accurate distance measurements and is not affected by lighting conditions, making it effective for detecting obstacles

and mapping the environment in low-light or nighttime scenarios.

- o **Limitations**: LiDAR can be expensive and is less effective at detecting small or transparent objects, such as pedestrians or glass.

3. **Radar**:
   - o **Radar** uses radio waves to detect the distance, speed, and direction of objects in the vehicle's vicinity. It is particularly useful for detecting objects at longer distances and in adverse weather conditions (e.g., rain, snow, fog), where cameras and LiDAR may struggle.
   - o **Advantages**: Radar works well in challenging weather conditions and can detect moving objects (e.g., other vehicles) even in low visibility conditions.
   - o **Limitations**: Radar does not provide detailed object recognition or depth information, making it less effective for identifying specific objects like pedestrians.

4. **Sensor Fusion**:
   - o By combining data from cameras, LiDAR, and radar, autonomous vehicles can create a more accurate and robust understanding of their environment. **Sensor fusion** combines the strengths of each sensor type, compensating for the limitations of others.

- o For instance, radar can detect the speed and location of a moving car, while LiDAR can provide detailed 3D information about the car's shape and surroundings. Cameras can then be used to recognize specific objects like pedestrians or traffic signs.
- o **Kalman filters** and **Bayesian fusion** methods are often used in sensor fusion to merge the data from multiple sensors and produce a single, unified model of the environment.

Real-World Example: Autonomous Navigation Systems in Tesla Cars

Tesla has become one of the most well-known companies developing autonomous driving systems. Tesla's **Autopilot** system and **Full Self-Driving (FSD)** capabilities rely heavily on computer vision, sensor fusion, and deep learning to navigate roads and perform tasks such as lane-keeping, adaptive cruise control, and automatic lane changes.

1. **Tesla's Perception System**:
   - o Tesla vehicles use **eight cameras**, **radar**, and **Ultrasonic sensors** for their perception system. The cameras provide 360-degree coverage around the vehicle, capturing images for object detection, lane recognition, and traffic light identification.

- o **Sensor Fusion** is used to combine the data from cameras, radar, and ultrasonic sensors to create a detailed map of the car's environment. For instance, the radar helps detect vehicles in front of the car, while cameras detect and classify objects like pedestrians and road signs.
- o Tesla does not use **LiDAR** in its vehicles, relying instead on a vision-based approach combined with deep learning algorithms for perception. Tesla believes that a vision-based system, similar to how humans drive using their eyes, is the best approach for achieving full autonomy.

2. **Training and Deep Learning**:
   - o Tesla's **neural networks** are trained using data collected from the fleet of vehicles on the road. Each Tesla vehicle sends anonymized driving data back to Tesla's servers, where it is used to improve the perception system and update the vehicle's software.
   - o Tesla uses this data to fine-tune the models for various tasks, such as detecting pedestrians, recognizing traffic signs, and understanding driving scenarios in different environments (e.g., city streets, highways).

3. **Autopilot and Full Self-Driving Features**:
   - o **Autopilot** offers features like **lane keeping**, **adaptive cruise control**, and **automatic lane changes**, where the

vehicle can navigate highways and adjust speed based on traffic conditions.
- o **Full Self-Driving (FSD)** includes advanced features such as **Navigate on Autopilot**, which allows the car to navigate highway exits and interchanges, and **Summon**, which allows the car to park itself in tight spaces.
4. **Challenges and Future of Tesla's Autonomous Driving**:
   - o While Tesla's Autopilot and Full Self-Driving systems have made significant progress, fully autonomous driving remains a work in progress. Challenges include improving performance in complex urban environments, ensuring safety in all driving conditions, and addressing regulatory and ethical concerns.
   - o Tesla continues to improve its systems through software updates and data-driven improvements, and it has the goal of achieving **Level 5 autonomy**, where no human intervention is required under any circumstances.

Summary

- **Computer vision** plays a critical role in enabling **autonomous vehicles** to perceive their surroundings, including detecting objects, recognizing lane markings, and understanding traffic conditions.

- **Sensor fusion** combines data from multiple sensors, such as **cameras**, **LiDAR**, and **radar**, to create a comprehensive view of the environment, helping autonomous vehicles navigate in complex and dynamic conditions.
- **Tesla's Full Self-Driving system** exemplifies how these technologies work together in real-world applications, using a vision-based approach combined with sensor fusion and deep learning.
- The development of autonomous vehicles is an ongoing process, with challenges remaining in terms of safety, regulatory approval, and achieving full autonomy.

CHAPTER 24

Edge Computing for Computer Vision

In this chapter, we will explore **edge computing** and its applications in **computer vision**. Edge computing refers to the practice of processing data closer to the source, such as on local devices, rather than sending data to centralized cloud servers for processing. This approach is particularly relevant in real-time applications where low latency, high throughput, and privacy are crucial. We will discuss the benefits of edge computing for computer vision, particularly for tasks like image recognition, and explore a **real-world example** of implementing image recognition on smartphones using **TensorFlow Lite**.

What is Edge Computing, and How Does it Apply to Computer Vision?

1. **Edge Computing Explained**:
   o **Edge computing** is the practice of processing data at the **edge** of the network, closer to where the data is generated, rather than relying on remote servers or cloud infrastructure. This is especially beneficial in scenarios where real-time decision-making, low latency, or resource constraints are important.
   o Instead of sending large volumes of data to a cloud server for processing (which

can introduce delays due to network bandwidth and server load), edge computing processes the data locally, on the device itself or a nearby local server.

2. **Application to Computer Vision**:
   - In **computer vision**, edge computing enables devices such as **smartphones, drones, cameras**, and **IoT (Internet of Things) devices** to process images and videos locally, without the need to send raw image data to the cloud for analysis.
   - **Advantages**:
     - **Low latency**: The ability to process images in real time directly on the device reduces the time between capturing an image and obtaining results (e.g., detecting an object or recognizing a face).
     - **Privacy**: Edge computing enhances privacy by processing sensitive data locally, reducing the need to transmit raw images to the cloud.
     - **Reduced bandwidth**: Since only processed information (such as the outcome of image recognition) is sent to the cloud, edge computing minimizes the amount of data that needs to be transmitted, reducing bandwidth usage and costs.

3. **Examples of Edge Devices**:

- o **Smartphones**: Mobile devices with powerful processors and cameras can handle image processing tasks for computer vision applications such as **face recognition**, **augmented reality**, and **image search**.
- o **Drones**: Drones equipped with cameras and local processing units can perform real-time image recognition for applications like **land surveying**, **wildlife monitoring**, and **delivery**.
- o **Smart Cameras**: Security cameras with onboard processing can detect intruders or recognize specific objects without needing a connection to the cloud.
- o **Autonomous Vehicles**: Self-driving cars use edge computing to process camera, LiDAR, and radar data locally, enabling real-time decision-making for navigation and safety.

Benefits of Processing Images on Local Devices (e.g., Mobile Phones, Drones)

1. **Real-Time Processing and Low Latency**:
   - o By processing images directly on the device, edge computing significantly reduces latency. This is especially important in applications where immediate decisions must be made, such as **object tracking**, **gesture recognition**, or **augmented reality**. For example, a drone flying in a complex environment

can process images locally to avoid obstacles in real time, without waiting for cloud-based processing.

2. **Energy Efficiency**:
   o Edge devices are often designed to be energy-efficient, as they need to operate for long periods (e.g., mobile phones or drones with limited battery life). Processing images on these devices reduces the need for constant communication with the cloud, saving energy and extending battery life.

3. **Improved Privacy and Security**:
   o Edge computing enhances **data privacy** by keeping sensitive information (such as personal images) on the local device, reducing the risk of data breaches. For example, facial recognition applications that process images on the phone can keep user data private without sending it to the cloud.
   o Additionally, local processing ensures that sensitive data never leaves the device, addressing privacy concerns associated with cloud-based computing.

4. **Reduced Network Dependency**:
   o Edge computing reduces reliance on internet connectivity, which is especially beneficial in areas with limited or no network access (e.g., remote locations, rural areas, or during travel). For instance, drones operating in remote environments can continue performing image

recognition tasks without needing a constant internet connection.

5. **Scalability**:
   o With edge computing, individual devices can handle image processing independently, reducing the load on cloud servers. This decentralized approach allows systems to scale more effectively, especially in applications that involve large numbers of devices (such as smart cameras or IoT sensors).

Real-World Example: Image Recognition on Smartphones Using TensorFlow Lite

One of the most popular applications of **edge computing** for computer vision is on **smartphones**. With the increasing power of mobile processors and specialized AI chips, smartphones can now handle complex computer vision tasks locally. **TensorFlow Lite** is a lightweight version of TensorFlow, designed specifically for running machine learning models on mobile and embedded devices.

1. **TensorFlow Lite**:
   o **TensorFlow Lite** is an open-source framework for running machine learning models on mobile and embedded devices. It is optimized for performance and small binary size, enabling models to run efficiently on devices with limited resources (e.g., smartphones and IoT devices).

236

- o TensorFlow Lite supports a variety of **pre-trained models** for image classification, object detection, and other computer vision tasks, which can be deployed on mobile devices for real-time processing.
2. **Image Recognition on Smartphones**:
   - o With TensorFlow Lite, mobile apps can perform **image classification**, **object detection**, and **pose estimation** directly on the device. For example, an image recognition app on a smartphone can classify objects (e.g., identifying animals in a photo) or detect faces in real-time without sending any data to the cloud.
3. **Example Use Case: Plant Disease Detection**:
   - o A **mobile app** can use TensorFlow Lite to process images of plants and detect diseases. The app can classify whether the plant is healthy or infected by recognizing visual patterns such as spots, discoloration, or other symptoms. This processing happens directly on the device, enabling instant feedback to the user without relying on an internet connection.
4. **Example Code: Using TensorFlow Lite for Image Classification on a Smartphone**:

Below is an outline of how image recognition can be implemented on a smartphone using TensorFlow Lite:

- **Step 1: Convert a TensorFlow model to TensorFlow Lite**: First, a trained TensorFlow model (e.g., an image classifier) is converted to TensorFlow Lite format using the TensorFlow Lite Converter.

```python
Copy
import tensorflow as tf

# Load a pre-trained TensorFlow model
model = tf.keras.applications.MobileNetV2(weights='imagenet')

# Convert the model to TensorFlow Lite format
converter = tf.lite.TFLiteConverter.from_keras_model(model)
tflite_model = converter.convert()

# Save the model
with open('mobilenet_v2.tflite', 'wb') as f:
    f.write(tflite_model)
```

- **Step 2: Load and Run the TensorFlow Lite Model on a Mobile Device**: On the mobile app, TensorFlow Lite is used to load and run the model locally for image classification.

```python
Copy
import tensorflow as tf
import numpy as np
from PIL import Image

# Load the TFLite model
interpreter =
tf.lite.Interpreter(model_p
ath="mobilenet_v2.tflite")
interpreter.allocate_tensor
s()

# Get input and output
details
input_details =
interpreter.get_input_detai
ls()
output_details =
interpreter.get_output_deta
ils()

# Load an image to classify
img =
Image.open('sample_image.jp
g').resize((224, 224))
input_data =
np.expand_dims(np.array(img
), axis=0)
```

```
# Set input tensor
interpreter.set_tensor(inpu
t_details[0]['index'],
input_data)

# Run inference
interpreter.invoke()

# Get output tensor
output_data             =
interpreter.get_tensor(outp
ut_details[0]['index'])

# Get predicted class
predicted_class         =
np.argmax(output_data)
print("Predicted    class:",
predicted_class)
```

In this code:

- o The pre-trained **MobileNetV2** model is converted to the TensorFlow Lite format.
- o The mobile device runs the model locally using TensorFlow Lite, processes an input image, and outputs the predicted class in real-time.

Summary

- **Edge computing** enables **real-time image recognition** and **low-latency processing** by performing computations on local devices, such as **smartphones**, **drones**, and **IoT devices**, rather than relying on cloud infrastructure.

- The benefits of edge computing for computer vision include **low latency**, **privacy**, **energy efficiency**, and **reduced bandwidth** usage.
- **TensorFlow Lite** allows for efficient deployment of machine learning models on mobile devices, enabling applications like **image recognition** directly on smartphones.
- We explored a **real-world example** of using TensorFlow Lite for **image classification** on mobile phones, demonstrating the power of edge computing in computer vision.

CHAPTER 25

The Future of Computer Vision

In this chapter, we will explore the **emerging trends** in computer vision and discuss how advances in **neural architecture search, self-supervised learning**, and **quantum computing** are shaping the future of image recognition technologies. We will also look at a **real-world example** of how these trends are likely to influence **AI-driven medical imaging** in the near future. By understanding these cutting-edge advancements, we can get a glimpse into the exciting possibilities for computer vision and its applications.

Emerging Trends in Computer Vision

1. **Neural Architecture Search (NAS)**:
    o **What is NAS?**
        ▪ **Neural Architecture Search (NAS)** is a technique used to automate the process of designing neural network architectures. Traditionally, designing the architecture of a neural network (e.g., the number of layers, type of layers, number of neurons) is a manual process that requires expert knowledge and trial-and-error.
        ▪ NAS aims to automate this process by using algorithms to search for the best architecture. This can

result in networks that are more efficient, accurate, and suited to specific tasks in computer vision.

- **How It Works**:
  - NAS typically uses **reinforcement learning** or **evolutionary algorithms** to explore the architecture space, evaluating various architectures and selecting the one that performs best on a given task (e.g., object detection, segmentation, etc.).
  - This automated approach helps optimize neural networks for a variety of tasks, leading to higher accuracy and more efficient models with fewer resources.

o **Example Use Cases**:
  - NAS can be used to design more efficient models for mobile devices, where computational resources are limited, or to optimize large-scale networks for tasks like **video analysis** or **autonomous driving**.
  - **MobileNet** and **EfficientNet** are examples of models that have been created using NAS, achieving high performance while being

lightweight enough for mobile deployment.

2. **Self-Supervised Learning (SSL)**:
   o **What is SSL?**
     - **Self-supervised learning** is a type of machine learning where the model learns from unlabeled data by generating its own labels or structure from the data itself. Unlike traditional supervised learning, where labeled data is required, SSL can leverage vast amounts of unlabeled data, which are often more readily available.
     - SSL works by creating pretext tasks that allow the model to learn useful representations from the input data, which can then be fine-tuned for downstream tasks (e.g., classification, detection).
     - **How It Works**:
       - A common approach in self-supervised learning is to predict parts of the data from other parts. For example, in image recognition, a model might be trained to predict missing parts of an image (image inpainting) or the spatial relationship between patches of an image (context prediction).

244

- Over time, the model learns to extract meaningful features from the data, which can then be applied to more specific tasks with fewer labeled examples.
  o **Benefits of SSL**:
    - **Scalability**: Self-supervised learning allows for the use of large, unlabeled datasets, reducing the need for costly manual annotation.
    - **Improved Generalization**: SSL enables the model to learn from diverse data sources and generalize better to new tasks or domains.
  o **Example Use Cases**:
    - SSL can be used in **image classification** tasks where labeled data is scarce, or in **video analysis** to learn representations of motion and context from unlabelled video data.
    - **OpenAI's CLIP** model is a prominent example of self-supervised learning in computer vision, capable of understanding images and texts without traditional labels.
3. **Vision Transformers (ViTs)**:
  o **What Are ViTs?**
    - **Vision Transformers (ViTs)** are a new architecture that has gained

significant attention in the field of computer vision. Instead of using convolutions (like CNNs), ViTs apply transformer networks (originally used in NLP) directly to image data.

- ViTs divide images into small patches and treat each patch as a token, much like how transformers process tokens in a sentence. This allows ViTs to capture long-range dependencies between different parts of an image, which can be beneficial for complex tasks like object detection and segmentation.

o **Benefits**:
- ViTs have shown to outperform traditional CNNs on large datasets and tasks that require global context, such as **image classification**.
- They offer better scalability to larger datasets and are seen as a promising direction for advancing computer vision models.

The Role of Quantum Computing in Image Recognition

1. **Quantum Computing Overview**:
   o **Quantum computing** leverages the principles of quantum mechanics to perform computations in ways that classical computers cannot. Quantum

computers use quantum bits (qubits), which can exist in multiple states simultaneously, allowing them to solve complex problems much faster than traditional computers.

2. **Potential Impact on Image Recognition**:
   o Quantum computing could revolutionize image recognition by dramatically speeding up the training and inference times for deep learning models, especially in tasks like **image classification**, **object detection**, and **3D vision**.
   o **Quantum-enhanced machine learning (QML)** techniques could be used to accelerate data processing, optimize training algorithms, and handle large datasets more efficiently, potentially reducing the need for extensive data labeling.
   o **Quantum Convolutional Networks (QCNNs)** are being explored as a potential extension of classical convolutional neural networks, with quantum computing offering the possibility of exponentially more efficient convolutions and feature extractions.

3. **Quantum Algorithms for Computer Vision**:
   o **Quantum algorithms** such as **quantum optimization** and **quantum Fourier transforms** could be applied to improve feature extraction, image compression, and real-time image processing.

- o **Quantum machine learning (QML)** techniques have the potential to enhance **self-supervised learning** by leveraging the ability of quantum computers to handle large and complex datasets more efficiently.
- o **Challenges**:
    - While quantum computing holds immense promise, current quantum machines are still in their early stages, and practical implementations of quantum-enhanced computer vision are not yet widespread.
    - The development of quantum algorithms for image recognition remains an area of active research, with many challenges to overcome in terms of hardware limitations and algorithm design.

Real-World Example: Predicting Future Trends in AI-Driven Medical Imaging

One of the most exciting applications of **AI-driven computer vision** is in **medical imaging**, where AI models assist doctors in diagnosing diseases, detecting abnormalities, and predicting health outcomes. These models are becoming increasingly advanced, with the potential to revolutionize the healthcare industry.

1. **Current Trends in AI-Driven Medical Imaging**:

- o **Automated Diagnostics**: AI models are being used to automatically analyze medical images, such as X-rays, MRIs, and CT scans, to identify diseases like cancer, heart conditions, and neurological disorders. These systems often outperform human radiologists in detecting certain conditions.
- o **Personalized Medicine**: AI-driven medical imaging systems are beginning to provide more personalized treatment recommendations by analyzing patient-specific data. For example, models can predict how tumors will respond to different treatments based on medical imaging data.

2. **Future Trends in AI and Medical Imaging**:
   - o **Self-Supervised Learning**: As self-supervised learning becomes more refined, it will allow AI models to learn from vast amounts of unlabeled medical data, making it easier to train diagnostic models even with limited labeled data. This will make AI-driven medical imaging more accessible and scalable.
   - o **Neural Architecture Search (NAS)**: NAS could lead to the development of more efficient and accurate models for medical imaging, enabling better detection of diseases with fewer resources.
   - o **Quantum Computing**: The combination of AI and quantum computing may allow

for faster processing of complex medical images, accelerating the development of real-time diagnostic systems for hospitals and clinics.

3. **Real-World Example: AI in Cancer Diagnosis**:
   - **Breast Cancer Detection**: AI systems, using **deep learning models** trained on large datasets of mammograms, have demonstrated the ability to identify early signs of **breast cancer** with high accuracy. These models can detect subtle changes in breast tissue that might go unnoticed by human radiologists, leading to earlier diagnosis and better patient outcomes.
   - **Skin Cancer Detection: Self-supervised learning** is also being applied to **dermatological images** for skin cancer detection. By training on large volumes of unlabeled images, AI models can learn to identify suspicious moles and lesions, improving early detection rates.

Summary

- **Emerging trends** in computer vision include **neural architecture search (NAS)**, **self-supervised learning (SSL)**, and **quantum computing**, which are transforming the field by enabling more efficient, scalable, and powerful image recognition systems.

- **Quantum computing** has the potential to revolutionize image recognition by speeding up processing times and improving data handling capabilities, although practical implementations are still in early development.
- In the realm of **medical imaging**, AI-driven systems are already making a significant impact, and future advancements in self-supervised learning, NAS, and quantum computing will continue to enhance diagnostic accuracy and efficiency.
- **AI-driven medical imaging** technologies are poised to revolutionize healthcare, improving early diagnosis and treatment outcomes for a wide range of conditions, from cancer detection to personalized medicine.

In the next chapter, we will explore **ethical considerations** in the development and deployment of AI models in real-world applications.

CHAPTER 26

Building a Computer Vision System from Scratch

In this chapter, we will walk through the **step-by-step process** of building a **complete image recognition system** from scratch. We'll explore the integration of multiple AI techniques and architectures, including data preprocessing, model training, evaluation, and deployment. Finally, we'll work through a **real-world project**: **creating a product recommendation system based on visual data**, which uses computer vision to analyze images of products and recommend similar items to users.

Step-by-Step Guide to Building a Complete Image Recognition System

1. **Step 1: Define the Problem and Gather Data**
   o Before building any system, it's essential to **define the problem** and understand what the model needs to recognize. For example, if we want to build an image recognition system to identify products in an e-commerce setting, the problem could be to **classify products** based on their images.
   o **Data Collection**: Image recognition models require large amounts of labeled data to train effectively. Data can be gathered from public datasets (e.g.,

ImageNet, **CIFAR-10**, or **COCO**) or custom datasets relevant to the problem domain.

- **Tip**: If the data is limited, consider data augmentation techniques (e.g., flipping, rotating, zooming) to artificially expand the dataset.

2. **Step 2: Preprocess the Data**

   o Data preprocessing is crucial to ensure that the images are in a format suitable for training. Common preprocessing steps include:

      - **Resizing**: Resize images to a consistent shape, typically 224x224 or 128x128 pixels.
      - **Normalization**: Normalize pixel values to a range between 0 and 1 or -1 and 1.
      - **Data Augmentation**: Apply random transformations (e.g., rotation, flipping, scaling) to simulate real-world variations and improve model robustness.

Example Code for Preprocessing:

```python
Copy
from
tensorflow.keras.preprocessing.image import ImageDataGenerator
```

```
from
tensorflow.keras.preprocessing
import image
import numpy as np

# Define data augmentation
strategies
datagen = ImageDataGenerator(
    rescale=1./255,
    rotation_range=20,
    width_shift_range=0.2,
    height_shift_range=0.2,
    shear_range=0.2,
    zoom_range=0.2,
    horizontal_flip=True,
    fill_mode='nearest'
)

# Load and preprocess an image
img                         =
image.load_img('product_image.jp
g', target_size=(224, 224))
img_array                   =
image.img_to_array(img)
img_array                   =
np.expand_dims(img_array,
axis=0)

# Apply data augmentation
augmented_images            =
datagen.flow(img_array)
```

3. **Step 3: Choose and Train a Model**

- There are many types of models for image recognition. For starters, you can use a **Convolutional Neural Network (CNN)**, which is highly effective for tasks like image classification, object detection, and segmentation.
  - **Basic CNN Architecture**: Build a simple CNN with convolutional layers, pooling layers, and fully connected layers.
  - **Pre-trained Models**: Consider using **transfer learning** with pre-trained models like **VGG16**, **ResNet**, or **MobileNet**. These models have been trained on large datasets and can be fine-tuned for your specific task.

Example Code for Building a Simple CNN:

```python
Copy
from      tensorflow.keras.models
import Sequential
from      tensorflow.keras.layers
import    Conv2D,    MaxPooling2D,
Flatten, Dense

# Build the CNN model
model = Sequential([
    Conv2D(32,       (3,        3),
activation='relu',
input_shape=(224, 224, 3)),
```

```
    MaxPooling2D(2, 2),
    Conv2D(64,        (3,       3),
activation='relu'),
    MaxPooling2D(2, 2),
    Flatten(),
    Dense(128,
activation='relu'),
    Dense(10,
activation='softmax')  # Assuming
10 classes for classification
])

# Compile the model
model.compile(optimizer='adam',
loss='categorical_crossentropy',
metrics=['accuracy'])
```

4. **Step 4: Train the Model**
   - Split the dataset into training, validation, and testing sets.
   - Train the model using the training data and validate it on the validation set.
   - Use **early stopping** and **model checkpoints** to prevent overfitting and save the best model during training.

Example Code for Training:

```python
Copy
#    Assuming    training    and
validation    data    are    in
```

```
directories        'train'        and
'validation'
train_generator                    =
datagen.flow_from_directory('tra
in',    target_size=(224,    224),
batch_size=32,
class_mode='categorical')
validation_generator              =
datagen.flow_from_directory('val
idation',        target_size=(224,
224),              batch_size=32,
class_mode='categorical')

# Train the model
model.fit(train_generator,
epochs=10,
validation_data=validation_gener
ator, verbose=2)
```

5. **Step 5: Evaluate the Model**
   o Once training is complete, evaluate the model on the test dataset to determine its performance on unseen data. Use metrics like **accuracy**, **precision**, **recall**, and **F1-score** to assess the model's effectiveness.
   o A **confusion matrix** can also be used to visualize the performance and errors of the classification model.

Example Code for Evaluation:

```
python
Copy
```

```
from    sklearn.metrics    import
confusion_matrix
import matplotlib.pyplot as plt

# Evaluate the model
test_loss,      test_acc      =
model.evaluate(test_generator)
print(f'Test            accuracy:
{test_acc}')

# Optionally, plot the confusion
matrix
y_true = test_generator.classes
y_pred                          =
model.predict(test_generator)
cm    =    confusion_matrix(y_true,
np.argmax(y_pred, axis=1))
plt.imshow(cm, cmap='Blues')
plt.show()
```

6. **Step 6: Model Deployment**
   - o Once the model is trained and evaluated, deploy it for use in real-world applications.
   - o For mobile or embedded devices, you can use frameworks like **TensorFlow Lite** or **ONNX** for efficient deployment on resource-constrained devices.

Example Code for Deploying with TensorFlow Lite:

```
python
```

```
Copy
# Convert model to TensorFlow
Lite format
converter                  =
tf.lite.TFLiteConverter.from_ker
as_model(model)
tflite_model               =
converter.convert()

# Save the converted model
with open('model.tflite', 'wb')
as f:
    f.write(tflite_model)
```

Integrating Multiple AI Techniques and Architectures

1. **Using Pre-trained Models (Transfer Learning)**:
   - Transfer learning allows you to leverage pre-trained models on large datasets like ImageNet and adapt them to your specific task. Fine-tuning a pre-trained model is an efficient way to build high-performing models with smaller datasets.

   Example: Fine-tuning a pre-trained **ResNet** model for product classification:

```
python
Copy
from
tensorflow.keras.applications
import ResNet50
```

```
from          tensorflow.keras.layers
import GlobalAveragePooling2D

# Load a pre-trained ResNet50
model       (without      the      top
classification layer)
base_model                         =
ResNet50(weights='imagenet',
include_top=False,
input_shape=(224, 224, 3))
x = base_model.output
x = GlobalAveragePooling2D()(x)
predictions       =        Dense(10,
activation='softmax')(x)     #   10
classes

model                              =
Model(inputs=base_model.input,
outputs=predictions)

# Fine-tune the model
for layer in base_model.layers:
    layer.trainable = False

model.compile(optimizer='adam',
loss='categorical_crossentropy',
metrics=['accuracy'])
```

2. **Ensemble Learning**:
   - Combining multiple models into an ensemble can improve the accuracy of the image recognition system. For example, you can combine different architectures

(e.g., CNNs, Vision Transformers) or combine models trained on different subsets of the data to improve performance.

3. **Object Detection**:
   - o For more advanced use cases, such as detecting and localizing objects in images (e.g., product detection in a shopping cart), you can use **object detection models** like **YOLO (You Only Look Once)** or **Faster R-CNN**. These models predict the location of objects in an image and classify them simultaneously.

Real-World Project: Creating a Product Recommendation System Based on Visual Data

Project Overview: We will create a product recommendation system that uses computer vision to recommend similar products based on visual features extracted from images. This system will analyze product images uploaded by users (or retrieved from a database) and suggest products with similar visual characteristics.

1. **Data Collection**: Collect product images from an e-commerce platform. For each product, collect the corresponding metadata, such as category, brand, and price.
2. **Image Feature Extraction**:
   - o Use a **pre-trained CNN model** (e.g., **ResNet50**) to extract features from the product images. These features will serve

as the basis for measuring similarity between products.

3. **Similarity Calculation**:
   o Use **cosine similarity** or **Euclidean distance** to calculate the similarity between the feature vectors of two products. The higher the similarity score, the more likely the products are visually similar.

4. **Recommendation Engine**:
   o Given a product image, the system will calculate its feature vector and recommend other products with similar visual features.

Example Code for Product Recommendation:

```python
Copy
from    sklearn.metrics.pairwise
import cosine_similarity
import numpy as np

# Assume product_features is a
list of feature vectors extracted
from product images
product_features              =
np.array([...])

# Given a query product feature
vector
query_feature = np.array([...])
```

```
# Calculate    cosine   similarity
between    the    query    and    all
products
similarities                =
cosine_similarity([query_feature
], product_features)

# Get  the  indices  of  the  most
similar products
similar_products            =
np.argsort(similarities[0])[::-
1]

print("Recommended    Products:",
similar_products)
```

Summary

- Building a complete image recognition system involves multiple steps, from **data collection** and **preprocessing** to **model training** and **deployment**.
- Integrating multiple AI techniques, including **pre-trained models**, **ensemble learning**, and **object detection**, can improve the performance of the system.
- In the **real-world project**, we demonstrated how to create a **product recommendation system** using visual data by extracting features from images and measuring their similarity to suggest similar products to users.

In the next chapter, we will dive into **advanced techniques** in **deep learning** for computer vision and explore their applications in **real-world systems**.

CHAPTER 27

Conclusion: The Path Forward in Computer Vision

As we reach the end of this book, let's take a moment to recap the **key concepts** and **techniques** covered, reflect on the advancements in **computer vision**, and explore how you can continue advancing your skills and apply computer vision to real-world projects. The field of computer vision is evolving rapidly, and there's always something new to learn. Whether you're just starting or already deep into building complex systems, this chapter will guide you toward **next steps** for your continued growth in this exciting area.

Recap of Key Concepts and Techniques Covered in the Book

1. **Introduction to Computer Vision**:
   o We began by exploring the foundational concepts of computer vision, including how machines interpret and process visual data. Key tasks such as **image classification**, **object detection**, **image segmentation**, and **activity recognition** were introduced.
2. **Core Machine Learning and Deep Learning Techniques**:
   o We discussed **machine learning** principles and how they apply to

computer vision, including supervised and unsupervised learning techniques.

- o We introduced **deep learning** models, particularly **Convolutional Neural Networks (CNNs)**, which have become the backbone of modern image recognition systems.

3. **Data Preparation and Model Development**:
- o Data collection, **preprocessing**, and **augmentation** were covered as essential steps in preparing data for training. These steps ensure that models can generalize effectively.
- o Building models using frameworks like **TensorFlow** and **Keras** was demonstrated, and we discussed training, evaluating, and fine-tuning models for optimal performance.

4. **Advanced Techniques**:
- o We covered advanced topics like **transfer learning**, **object detection** with models like YOLO and Faster R-CNN, and techniques for handling complex tasks such as **image segmentation** using architectures like Mask R-CNN.
- o We also explored emerging areas like **self-supervised learning**, **neural architecture search**, and **quantum computing** in the context of computer vision, illustrating how these developments are shaping the future of the field.

5. **Real-World Applications**:

- o Throughout the book, we provided real-world examples, such as **autonomous vehicles**, **medical imaging**, **security surveillance**, and **augmented reality**, to show how computer vision is transforming industries.
- o The final section focused on **building a computer vision system from scratch**, guiding you through every stage from data collection to model deployment, and using **image recognition** for a product recommendation system.

How to Stay Updated in the Field of Computer Vision

The field of computer vision is rapidly evolving, and staying updated is essential for keeping your skills sharp and applying the latest techniques. Here are some strategies to keep up:

1. **Follow Research Papers and Conferences**:
   - o The latest breakthroughs in computer vision are often published in academic papers. Key conferences to follow include:
     - **CVPR (Conference on Computer Vision and Pattern Recognition)**
     - **ICCV (International Conference on Computer Vision)**
     - **ECCV (European Conference on Computer Vision)**

- **NeurIPS (Conference on Neural Information Processing Systems)** for deep learning research.
  - Websites like **arXiv.org** and **Google Scholar** provide access to cutting-edge research papers.

2. **Engage with the Computer Vision Community**:
   - Join online communities, forums, and social media groups dedicated to computer vision, such as:
     - **Reddit's r/computervision**
     - **Stack Overflow** for solving technical issues and learning from the community.
     - **Twitter**: Follow influential researchers, companies, and organizations like OpenAI, Tesla, and Google AI to stay informed.

3. **Online Courses and Tutorials**:
   - Continuously learning from online courses and tutorials is key to staying updated. Platforms like **Coursera, Udacity, Fast.ai**, and **edX** offer specialized courses in computer vision and deep learning.
   - **YouTube** channels like **Two Minute Papers** or **DeepLizard** also provide quick overviews of recent advancements.

4. **Read Books and Blogs**:
   - Books like **"Deep Learning" by Ian Goodfellow**, **"Deep Learning for**

Computer Vision" by **Rajalingappaa Shanmugamani**, and other authoritative texts in the field provide in-depth knowledge.

- o **Blogs** and technical articles from industry leaders (like **TensorFlow blog**, **PyTorch blog**, or **Distill.pub**) are great for understanding practical implementations and new trends.

5. **Participate in Competitions**:
   - o Engage in **Kaggle** competitions or **GitHub** repositories related to computer vision projects. Competitions often push the limits of what is possible in computer vision and expose you to real-world challenges and solutions.
   - o Participate in **hackathons** or collaborate with others on open-source computer vision projects.

Next Steps for Advancing Your Skills and Applying Computer Vision in Real-World Projects

1. **Deepen Your Knowledge of Neural Networks and AI Architectures**:
   - o To stay ahead, dive deeper into more advanced architectures like **Vision Transformers (ViTs)** and **Generative Adversarial Networks (GANs)**. Exploring these will give you insights into the cutting-edge innovations in computer vision.
2. **Explore Domain-Specific Applications**:

- o Identify specific domains where you can apply your computer vision skills. This could be in **healthcare, e-commerce, autonomous systems, robotics,** or **augmented reality**.
- o For example, you could focus on **AI-driven medical imaging**, where computer vision is used for early detection of diseases, or **smart cities**, where it can be applied to surveillance and urban planning.

3. **Build Real-World Projects**:
   - o Put your knowledge to practice by creating real-world computer vision projects. Build systems that solve problems you're passionate about, such as:
     - **Image classification** for social media platforms.
     - **Object detection** in autonomous drones or delivery robots.
     - **Augmented reality apps** using image recognition to overlay digital content on physical environments.

4. **Collaborate with Industry Professionals**:
   - o Partner with professionals working on large-scale computer vision projects. Join open-source communities, contribute to research papers, or work with companies developing cutting-edge products. This will allow you to gain valuable

experience and contribute to impactful projects.

5. **Master Tools and Frameworks**:
   - Familiarize yourself with popular computer vision libraries and frameworks like **OpenCV**, **TensorFlow**, **PyTorch**, and **Keras**. These tools are essential for building efficient and scalable systems.
   - Additionally, learn about cloud platforms and **edge computing** techniques for deploying models on devices like smartphones, drones, and IoT devices.

6. **Stay Curious and Experiment**:
   - Computer vision is a dynamic field with constant advancements. Don't be afraid to experiment with new models, datasets, or application areas. Try building something that excites you and see how you can apply cutting-edge methods to solve real problems.

Summary

In this book, we have explored the foundational and advanced concepts of computer vision, from basic **image classification** to complex topics like **neural architecture search**, **self-supervised learning**, and **quantum computing**. Along the way, we have examined real-world applications, provided practical tutorials, and offered insights into how these technologies are transforming industries from healthcare to autonomous driving.

As you move forward in your computer vision journey:

- Keep learning from research papers, courses, and industry professionals.
- Continue building hands-on projects to apply your knowledge.
- Stay curious, experiment with new ideas, and strive to make meaningful contributions to the field.

The future of computer vision is bright, with endless possibilities for innovation. Whether you're aiming to build the next breakthrough product, improve the healthcare landscape, or enhance autonomous systems, computer vision will be at the heart of it all. We look forward to seeing how you use these tools to shape the future.

www.ingramcontent.com/pod-product-compliance
Lightning Source LLC
LaVergne TN
LVHW022338060326
832902LV00022B/4100